Queen Elizabeth I is perhaps the most famous monarch in English history. The achievements of the nation she ruled, in exploration, in war, and in the arts, were such that ever since, men have looked back on her reign (1558–1603) as a golden age. The Queen herself, however, remains an enigma. She trod delicately and surely through the pitfalls of the strife between Catholics and Protestants, the constant threat of invasion from Spain, and the demands of Parliament for a say in government. What were the qualities that enabled her to succeed where so many might have failed?

Alan Kendall tells how, as the focus of a series of intrigues and rebellions, she learned early in life to watch her political step if she wished to avoid the fate of her mother, Anne Boleyn, at the hands of the executioner. He explains her decision that for England's sake she must not get married, either to a subject like the Earl of Leicester or to a foreign monarch such as King Eric of Sweden. He describes how her political realism slowly overcame her moral scruples, and made her agree to the execution of her cousin Mary Queen of Scots. He displays her in her hour of triumph, after the defeat of the Spanish Armada. Finally he paints a rather sad picture of her in old age, losing her political touch and coming close to losing the love of her people.

Through the lavish use of contemporary illustrations and quotations, this book gives a vivid picture of an all-powerful Queen who could never quite reconcile her personal feelings with her judgement as a sovereign.

NON SINE SOLE
IRIS.

Elizabeth I

Alan Kendall

St. Martin's Press/New York
Wayland Publishers Limited/Hove, England

Copyright © 1975 by Wayland Publishers Limited
First published in the UK in 1975 by
Wayland Publishers Limited, 49 Lansdowne Place,
Hove, Sussex BN3 1HS
SBN 85340 391 0

First published in the USA in 1977
All rights reserved. For information, write:
St. Martin's Press, Inc., 175 Fifth Avenue,
New York, N.Y. 10010
Library of Congress Catalog Card Number: 77-288

Printed in Great Britain by
Tinling (1973) Ltd

Library of Congress Cataloging in Publication Data
Kendall, Alan.
  Elizabeth I.

  Bibliography: p.
  Includes index.
  SUMMARY: A biography of Elizabeth I, who secured her
claim to the English throne by executing her cousin,
Mary Stuart, Queen of the Scots.

  1. Elizabeth, Queen of England, 1533-1603—Juvenile
literature. 2. Great Britain—Kings and rulers—Biography—
Juvenile literature. 3. Great Britain—History—
Elizabeth, 1558-1603—Juvenile literature. [1. Elizabeth,
Queen of England, 1533-1603. 2. Queens.
3. Great Britain—History—Elizabeth, 1558-1603]
I. Title.
DA355.K46 1977   942.05'5'0924 [B] [92]   77-288
ISBN 0-312-24247-6

Contents

1   A Dangerous Childhood   7
2   Queen Mary   13
3   Church and State   16
4   Into Europe?   20
5   The Queen of Scots   25
6   Proposals of Marriage   28
7   The Dutch Revolt   35
8   Death of a Queen   38
9   The Great Armada   42
10   Catholics and Puritans   49
11   Elizabeth and Essex   57
12   Power and Poverty   61
13   Painters, Musicians and Poets   68
14   Society: Problems of Progress   76
15   The New Century   81
16   Time for a change   87
    Principal Characters   90
    Table of Dates   92
    Picture Credits   94
    Further Reading   95
    Index   96

1 A Dangerous Childhood

ON 17TH NOVEMBER, 1558, Elizabeth Tudor became Queen of England. She inherited the throne of a country troubled by grave problems. Mary, the previous Queen and Elizabeth's half-sister, had left England financially ruined and on the brink of war with France. Many people expected civil war to break out between Catholics and Protestants. On 23rd November, when Elizabeth arrived in London, she feared that at any moment rebellion might break out, with the aim of overthrowing her and placing Mary Stuart, daughter-in-law of the King of France, on the throne. But from then on, all was pageantry, feasting and celebration in the streets of London. By the time of her coronation, on 15th January, 1559, Elizabeth had won the hearts of the citizens. Some years later, the historian Raphael Holinshed wrote, "After all the stormy, tempestuous and blustering windy weather of Queen Mary was overthrown, and the palpable fogs and mist of the most intolerable misery consumed, it pleased God to send England a quiet and calm season, and a world of blessings by good Queen Elizabeth." Perhaps he dared say nothing else, if he valued his life; but even after Elizabeth's death, there were few who disagreed with him. For over two centuries after her death, 17th November, the day of her accession, was celebrated in towns and villages throughout England with feasts, sports and bonfires in memory of Good Queen Bess.

Elizabeth Tudor was born on Sunday, 7th September, 1533, at Greenwich Palace, London. The original building – known as Placentia – has long since disappeared beneath the site of Sir Christopher Wren's

Opposite Princess Elizabeth, aged about twelve.
Below Elizabeth's birthplace, Greenwich Palace, on the Thames.

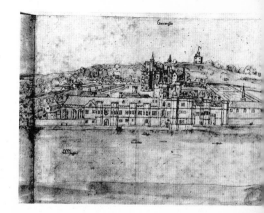

7

Henry VIII and Anne Boleyn, Elizabeth's parents, painted at about the time of her birth.

Royal Naval College, but a surviving engraving shows a typical rambling, late-medieval structure.

Elizabeth's mother was Anne Boleyn, the second wife of Henry VIII. The King had divorced his first wife, Katherine of Aragon, and badly wanted a son and heir. He was so angry at the birth of another daughter that he refused to go to the christening ceremony. The Ambassador from the Holy Roman Empire remarked: "God has forgotten him entirely, hardening him in his obstinacy to punish and ruin him."

Until Henry VIII's time, the church in England had been under the control of the Pope in Rome. The King had to accept the Pope's authority in matters of religion – and then, religion played a much bigger part in everyday life than it does now. When Henry wanted his marriage to Katherine declared void, he had to ask permission from the Pope, Clement VII. Clement was at that time virtually a prisoner of Katherine's nephew, the Holy Roman Emperor Charles V, and was ordered to refuse Henry's request. At that, Henry decided to defy the Pope's authority altogether, and declared himself Supreme Head of the Church of England.

During the same period, Martin Luther and his followers in Germany had attacked the Pope's position in matters of religious belief. They had begun by questioning his right to grant indulgences, or pardons for sins, and had gone on to attack the Catholic doctrine that it was necessary to observe the ceremonies of the Church and pray to God with the help of a priest. Henry VIII was certainly not a Lutheran, or Protestant, as they came to be called; but it was natural that Luther's ideas should come to take root in a country where the Papal authority had been successfully overthrown.

So Elizabeth became the living symbol of the break between England and Catholic Europe. For many years to come she was to live under the threat that many people wanted to remove her and restore the old religious order. In the end it was because she was so plainly English, unlike her half-sister Mary, that she became so well-loved by her fellow-countrymen.

Early in December 1533 the infant Elizabeth was sent away from London, and the dangers of plague, to the purer countryside air of Hatfield in Hertfordshire. Soon Mary, Katherine of Aragon's daughter, then almost eighteen, was sent to be maid of honour to the baby Elizabeth, and was deprived of her title of Princess of Wales. Henry VIII claimed that he had never been legally married to Katherine, therefore Mary was illegitimate and had no right to be the next Queen. He was determined to destroy all links with the Catholic past.

In January, 1536, Anne Boleyn gave birth prematurely to a boy, but it was stillborn. She was accused of having been unfaithful to Henry, and was executed the following May. The very next day Henry married Jane Seymour. In July Elizabeth was degraded to the same status as Mary. At last, the following year, a son was born. It is hard to know how Elizabeth felt towards the young Prince Edward, since at this time she saw very little of him or of her father. It was during this period of neglect that Elizabeth began to show her aptitude for learning that was one day to make her one of the most talented princesses of the sixteenth century.

In 1543, King Henry married his sixth and last wife, Catherine Parr. Catherine was a highly educated woman, who took her stepdaughter's welfare to heart. The earliest surviving letter we have by Elizabeth – in Italian – is to Catherine, dated 31st July, 1544. Elizabeth was then eleven years old. The earliest known portrait, which also dates from this period and is now in Windsor Castle, shows Elizabeth holding a book, beside a reading desk bearing a large open volume. The little Princess worked hard, and these were the most settled years of her childhood. The knowledge she gained then helped her in two crucial ways in the future. Her reading of the Bible and the works of the early Church fathers such as St. Augustine, usually in the original language, gave her a deep knowledge of the issues at stake during the Reformation. This helped her

"My sister Elizabeth is in good health and, thanks be to our Lord, such a child toward as I doubt not your Highness shall have cause to rejoice of in time coming." *Mary Tudor to Henry VIII, before Anne Boleyn's execution.*

"Her maidenly apparel made the noblemen's daughters and wives to be ashamed to be dressed and painted like peacocks. She never meddled with money but against her will, but . . . thought to touch it was to defile her pure hands consecrated to turn over good books, to lift up unto God in prayer and to deal alms to the poor." *John Aylmer, An Harborowe for Faithfull and Trewe Subjects, 1559.*

when she came to the throne and was faced with the problem of setting up a Church that as many as possible of her subjects would accept. Secondly, her fluency in languages enabled her to talk with ambassadors, read despatches and write letters without having to use interpreters or secretaries. She never left England – not even to visit Wales.

When Henry VIII died in 1547 and the boy king Edward VI came to the throne, Elizabeth went on living with her stepmother in Chelsea. Because King Edward was only nine, Edward Seymour, Duke of

Below Bishop Hugh Latimer, later burned at the stake under Queen Mary, preaching in front of Edward VI, who listens from the window, right.

Somerset, took charge of the Government as Lord Protector. Soon Catherine Parr married Thomas Seymour, Lord High Admiral and the Protector's brother. There were unpleasant rumours, however, that Elizabeth and Admiral Seymour were living together as lovers. Although this was quite untrue, in 1548 she left to set up her own household at Cheshunt, in Hertfordshire, with Kate Ashley as her governess. After Catherine died, Admiral Seymour plotted with Mistress Ashley to marry Elizabeth and use her to oust his brother as Protector. But he was arrested and taken to the Tower. Elizabeth only saved herself from the same fate by refusing to admit anything, and maintaining her innocence.

In the autumn of 1549 Edward Seymour himself was toppled from his place as Lord Protector by John Dudley, Earl of Warwick (and from 1551 Duke of Northumberland). Elizabeth was the centre of much of Dudley's plotting, since King Edward was a very sickly child who was not expected to survive for long. Dudley considered forcing Elizabeth to marry his son Guildford. In the event Guildford Dudley married Lady Jane Grey, and the young King was tricked into signing a document which altered the succession in Lady Jane's favour. Four days after Edward died, on 6th July, 1553, Lady Jane Grey was proclaimed Queen. Northumberland had badly underestimated how much support there was in the country for Mary, the legitimate successor, and within a fortnight his plot had collapsed. Elizabeth waited anxiously at Hatfield to see which way the tide of public opinion would turn.

> **"This day died a man with much wit, and very little judgement."**
> *Attributed to Elizabeth on hearing of the execution of Admiral Seymour.*

2 Queen Mary

AT THE AGE OF TWENTY Elizabeth now found herself heir to the throne of England. Between her and the crown was the new Queen, Mary, a fanatical Roman Catholic, who at thirty-seven was unmarried and seemingly doomed to become an old maid. Mary, however, planned to marry Philip, heir to the throne of Spain, and this, coupled with her restoration of the Roman Catholic rite in England, soon lost her the little popularity she had enjoyed.

The younger, Protestant and wholly English Princess thus became the focal point of the discontent which now appeared among large sections of the people. Mary was herself the daughter of a Spanish princess, and so any child of her marriage to Philip of Spain would be three-quarters Spanish. Spain, under the Emperor Charles V, who also ruled Austria, Holland and South America, was by far the most powerful country in Europe. No matter how sorry some people were for the way Mary had been treated in the past, they would rather have an English monarch any time, and there was just such a person in the young Princess Elizabeth. Elizabeth had already learned to cope with this situation and to avoid sharing Lady Jane Grey's fate. Even so, she came perilously close to disaster.

At first Mary treated Elizabeth well, as befitted her rank, but it was clear that in religious matters there would be trouble. Mary tried many times to make her half-sister worship as a Roman Catholic. At last Elizabeth agreed to go to Mass on 8th September, the Nativity of the Blessed Virgin Mary, but when the day dawned she pretended to be ill, and only went to church

Opposite Queen Mary and her husband Philip II of Spain, painted in 1558 in Whitehall Palace.

"God so turned the hearts of the people to her and against the Council [*i.e. Northumberland's supporters*] that she overcame them without bloodshed, notwithstanding there was made great expedition against her both by sea and land." *John Knox on the accession of Mary Tudor, 1553.*

John Bradford and John Leaf, two
Protestants, about to be burned at
the stake in Smithfield, London, in
1555.

"wearing a suffering air." She was not a regular
attender, even then, and Mary naturally had doubts
about Elizabeth's sincerity. Elizabeth in turn claimed
that she obeyed the dictates of her conscience, and was
not trying to stir up opposition to the Queen. Even so,
she felt uncomfortable at court, and asked leave to go
to Ashridge in Middlesex at the beginning of December.
She no doubt hoped that out of sight would mean out
of mind. On the way she sent Mary a letter asking for
"copes, chasubles, chalices and other ornaments for her
chapel." Mary could scarcely have been taken in.

England's discontent with Mary's efforts to overturn
the Reformation and bring back Roman Catholicism
exploded on 25th January, 1554. Sir Thomas Wyatt the
Younger, son of Henry VIII's court poet, called on the
men of Kent to revolt and led a march as far as
Southwark, across the Thames from London. Risings
in other parts of the country had been planned, but
these came to nothing, and the rebellion was defeated.
Elizabeth was summoned to court, since Mary sus-
pected her of conspiring with the rebels. In fact,
although she would no doubt have liked Wyatt to
succeed, she had not been involved in the plot. In
March, after Wyatt's trial, she was sent to the Tower of
London. Nothing could be proved against her, though,
and Mary realized she could not keep her half-sister in
prison indefinitely. Elizabeth had to be out of the way
by the time Philip II arrived for the wedding, since her
presence might lead to protests, so Mary at last decided
to send her to Woodstock House, near Oxford.

While at Woodstock, Elizabeth outwardly conformed
to the Catholic faith, though she still had the litany and
some of the Mass said in English, until the Queen found
out about this. Once again, Elizabeth had to promise
that she would obey, but few people were convinced
that she had really been won over. Meanwhile, Mary
began to persecute those Protestants who made no
secret of their beliefs. Many hundreds were burned at
the stake at Smithfield, in London, and in other towns
and villages throughout England. Mary thus lost all

hope of gaining popular support for her policies.

Shortly after Easter 1555, Mary summoned Elizabeth to Hampton Court, and the two sisters became friends again. In the succeeding months they were probably as close as they ever were in the whole of their lives. Elizabeth then divided her time between the court and Hatfield, and though not entirely at liberty, she enjoyed a good measure of freedom. Things continued to worsen for Mary, however. Philip II went back to Spain, and Mary failed to give birth to the long hoped-for child. She was drawn into supporting her husband in his war against France, as a result of which Calais – the last piece of English territory on the continent of Europe – was lost.

Instead of increasing England's prestige by marrying Philip of Spain, Mary had brought it to the lowest point anyone could remember. During the autumn of 1558 her health began to decline, and in the early hours of 17th November she died. Philip of Spain's special envoy, Count de Feria, had arrived in England at the beginning of the month, assuming that Spanish authority would be established in England. Of the new Queen, however, he had to report to his master: "She seems to me incomparably more feared than her sister, and gives her orders and has her way as absolutely as her father did."

Thomas Cranmer, Archbishop of Canterbury, thrusts his hand first into the flames, because he has used it to sign a document recanting his Protestant faith.

"There came to me, whom I did both hear and see, one Isabel Malt [who] being delivered of a man-child upon Whit Sunday in the morning, which was the eleventh day of June, anno 1555, there came to her the Lord North, and another lord to her unknown . . . demanding of her if she would part with her child, and would swear that she never knew nor had any such child." *John Foxe (1516–87), Acts and Monuments of the Church. It was widely believed that Queen Mary had actually given birth to a child in 1555. This was perhaps an attempt to provide tangible evidence, though Foxe was an extreme Protestant who may have invented the tale.*

3 Church and State

Salutes being fired from ships, churches and the Tower in honour of Elizabeth's triumphal entry into London.

WHEN ELIZABETH CAME TO THE THRONE her most urgent task was to settle the religious question. Mary's return to Catholicism, and especially her burning at the stake of Protestants who refused to conform, had bitterly angered many people. Now too, the Protestants who had gone into exile in Switzerland during Mary's reign returned full of the teachings of John Calvin of Geneva. Calvin believed that each individual was predestined at birth either to be saved or to be damned. This left little room for the Catholic doctrine of "justification by works".

The very first law passed by Elizabeth's first Parliament was the Act of Supremacy, which restored a modified version of her father's Act of 1534. By this Act Elizabeth was declared "only supreme governor of this realm . . . as well in all spiritual or ecclesiastical things or causes as temporal." This was followed by the Act of Uniformity, which brought back the forms of worship in use in the Church under Henry VIII, and the Prayer Book of 1552, with a few changes designed to win over the Catholics.

It is hard to see what Elizabeth's own religious views were. Although she had worshipped as a Catholic during her sister's reign, she was certainly a Protestant at heart. Yet to say that her settlement of the religious question was just a compromise, a middle way between Catholicism and Protestantism, is to simplify too much. Elizabeth's settlement achieved a balance between two extremes – Protestant theology on one hand and Catholic ritual on the other – and in this way skilfully managed to unite in a single church tendencies which, if either one of them had been allowed to take control, would have turned large sections of the nation against the state.

At the start of the reign, four bishoprics were vacant, and five bishops died within a year. Of those who were in office, many of them Catholics appointed by Mary, all but one refused to accept Elizabeth's settlement, and they were deprived of their sees. They wrote to the Queen on 4th December, 1559, and she replied two days later in terms which make very clear how she intended to handle the matter of religion: "As to your entreaty for us to listen to you, we wave it: yet do return you this our answer. . . . We give you warning, that for the future we hear no more of this kind, lest you provoke us to execute those penalties enacted for the punishing of our resisters: which out of our clemency we have forborne." The body of the letter reveals a deep knowledge of religious history, and the ability to use the

A painting given by the Queen as a present to her minister Sir Francis Walsingham, showing her introducing the Goddess of Peace to Britain in place of Philip and Mary's God of War.

William Cecil, Lord Burghley, Elizabeth's Secretary of State.

"The Church hath power to decree Rites or Ceremonies, and authority in Controversies of Faith: And yet it is not lawful for the Church to ordain any thing that is contrary to God's word Written, neither may it so expound one place of Scripture, that it be repugnant to another."
Article of Religion XX, Book of Common Prayer.

Scriptural arguments quoted by the bishops equally well to prove the Queen's own case.

One can see Elizabeth's settlement, then, as a reflection of her own personal outlook within the limits of what she believed the state of the country could reasonably allow. She could not heal the breach with Rome, because it would have meant accepting that her father's divorce was illegal and therefore that she was illegitimate. Nor was it possible to return to the fires of Smithfield of the previous reign, or go even further back and undo the dissolution of the monasteries. In any case, there were plenty of Catholics who had profited from having bought the confiscated monastic lands. On the other hand, Elizabeth was morally obliged to do something for the Protestants who had plotted and suffered on her behalf during Mary's reign, and the Protestants were her most loyal subjects. They were also some of the richest, most energetic and most learned, and she knew that both she and England needed them.

Elizabeth only insisted on outward conformity from those who opposed her religious settlement. As she herself put it, she did not want to "make windows into men's souls." Moreover, she hated extremists of any sort. She had no time for the ultra-Protestants. These extremists were fond of preaching, which she believed to be dangerous. They were also against bishops, who were appointed by the Queen and whose authority Elizabeth therefore saw as a prop to the monarchy and a means of keeping a hand on the reins of the Church.

During the early part of her reign, she had no quarrel with those Catholics who refrained from parading their religion in public. If she changed later, it was because events forced her to it. Not until the arrival of the Queen of Scots in England, the Rising in the North and the Papal Excommunication of Elizabeth in 1570 were her Catholic subjects forced to decide between their faith and their sovereign. Between two and three hundred men died, but in forty-five years of Elizabeth's reign, there were fewer executions for religious reasons than

The Orthodox true Minister,   the Seducer and false Prophet.

in less than three years of Mary's reign. Elizabeth only ever burned four men for their beliefs, and they were Anabaptists, believers in total social equality, who would have perished under any Christian regime.

As a measure of the success of Elizabeth's church settlement, it must be remembered that the vicious and crippling religious civil wars which broke out in France and the Netherlands at this time were avoided in England. The roots of conflict were not destroyed, but meanwhile the country had time to prosper and expand.

A cartoon showing a Church of England minister preaching to a calm and disciplined congregation, while a Puritan rants from a window to a disorderly mob.

4 Into Europe?

ANOTHER TASK FOR ELIZABETH early in her reign was to help England survive the terrible psychological shock of having lost Calais, the last outpost of her medieval empire in Europe. In 1559 she made peace with the King of France by the Treaty of Cateau-Cambrésis, under which England's right to Calais was recognized, but the town was to be held by the French for eight years. If it were not handed back then, the King of France should pay 500,000 crowns. At this point the King, Henri II, died and was succeeded first by his son François II (the husband of Mary Queen of Scots), and then at his death in 1560 by François' ten-year-old brother Charles IX. During the previous few years, Protestantism had spread into France from the little republic of Geneva, in Switzerland; now, the Catholic Church, which had begun to weed out the abuses that the Protestants had complained of, began to strike back all over Europe.

In France, Catherine de' Medici, Charles' mother, had the Pope's support for a campaign of persecution against the Huguenots, or French Protestants. Elizabeth began to increase the strength of her army and navy, and in 1562 sent six thousand men over to Normandy to help the Huguenots. Neither side wanted the English to interfere, so the Protestants made peace with their King and then turned on the English garrison at Le Havre, which Elizabeth was forced to surrender. This failure showed that open involvement in Europe was not wise for England, certainly not at such an early point in Elizabeth's reign. England could not raise a large enough army to compete with the European powers, and relied on her navy for security. In any case,

"On Thursday, began one other battery to the castle; which being a high and weak wall without ramparts, was made [as-]saultable the same day. Whereupon, the Captain of the Castle desired some more help to defend this breach, or else to know what my Lord thought best in that behalf. Then, after long debating, my Lord determined to have the towers overthrown, which one Saulle took upon him to do; notwithstanding, I said openly that 'if the castle were abandoned, it should be the loss of the town.'"

An account by John Highfield, Master of the Ordnance, of the loss of Calais, 1558.

"A Hieroglyphic of Britain," from John Dee's *Art of Navigation*, 1577. Elizabeth is shown presiding over the achievements of the English, symbolized by scenes from history and mythology.

negotiations were going on to find a French husband for the Queen. These might have been successful had it not been for the massacre of the Huguenots on St. Bartholomew's Eve in 1572. This made the prospect of a French Catholic consort for Elizabeth unacceptable to her Protestant subjects, certainly for the time being.

Elizabeth saw that she had far more to gain – both for England and for herself – by standing apart from Europe, and offering her services as a mediator. She could gain more, at much less cost, from internal trouble in Scotland, France and the Spanish Empire than from direct involvement. She might have become Queen of the Netherlands when the Dutch began to throw off Spanish domination, but she declined. Protestant Europe came to look to her for leadership, and morally she gave it, but she managed to do so without endangering England's safety. This was not simply a matter of policy: Elizabeth seems to have had a genuine desire for peace. As she told Parliament in 1593: "It might be thought simplicity in me that all this time of my reign I have not sought to advance my territories and enlarge my dominions; for opportunity hath served me to do it . . . my mind was never to invade my neighbours, or to usurp over any. I am content to reign over mine own, and to rule as a just prince."

Yet this desire for peace, both at home and abroad, had its drawbacks. There were some nettles which Elizabeth ought to have grasped, and did not. Her relationship with Parliament was one notable example. In failing to define its part in governing the country she left a major problem for her successors, which they were not fitted to resolve.

The Civil War of 1642–45 came about largely because the characters of James I and Charles I made them unable to compromise with the demands of the House of Commons for a greater say in government. If Elizabeth, who was much better liked by her M.P.s, had been able to do so, she would have done her successors and the nation a great service. As it was, she was content to manage Parliament, to storm, to flatter, to cajole – almost anything to get her own way. She generally managed to make ends meet, so she never felt any need to put the financial affairs of the crown on a permanently sound basis. This was to be a future royal Achilles' heel. The monarch needed Parliament to obtain money. During Elizabeth's reign, Parliament learned that its control over taxation could be used as a lever to obtain its demands for a say in government policy.

Even so, Elizabeth's handling of Parliament was masterly. There were certain matters, for instance whether she should marry, she felt it was not proper for M.P.s to discuss, and she did not hesitate to say so. If Parliament then persisted, she might have to yield a little, but she usually made her point. She summed up

"The Queen has reigned already twenty-six years, and during her reign Parliament has never been held. This year she enters her fifty-third year, as it is said, and she has sent orders through the whole realm to convoke Parliament. The principal cause is, I am told, that the English do not wish the King of Scotland, who is the next to the throne, to be King of England, and wish to know who after the Queen's death is to wear the crown."

Leopold von Wedel, A Journey through England and Scotland, 1584–85. Von Wedel was mistaken in his belief that Elizabeth had never summoned Parliament before.

this rather unusual three-sided relationship between God, herself and Parliament – representing the people – in her famous Golden Speech (see page 83). God had made her Queen, and therefore she ruled by Divine Right. At the same time she knew that she only ruled by the goodwill of her people. It was her particular genius that made such a curious and fragile relationship work.

Elizabeth seated in the House of Lords at the opening of Parliament.

The Chancellors Seat.

MARIA

G

SCOTIA
SSIMA REGINA
ANCIÆ DOTARIA
ANNO
ÆTATIS REGNIQ
36
ANCLICÆ CAPTIVÆ
10
S H
1578

5 The Queen of Scots

A PROBLEM WHICH FACED ELIZABETH soon after her accession, and would do for twenty-five years, was that of the Kingdom of Scotland, and in particular its Queen. Mary Queen of Scots was the only daughter of James V of Scotland and the French Princess Mary of Guise. Mary's father died in the same year that she was born, and she became Queen, with her mother ruling as regent. At the age of six she was sent to France to be educated, and in 1558 she married the Dauphin, François. When Mary Tudor died, Mary and François claimed the throne of England by Mary's descent from Margaret Tudor, daughter of Henry VII and mother of James V. François became King of France in 1559, but died the following year. In August 1561 Mary came home to Scotland to take possession of her kingdom. In the lowlands of Scotland, many people had been converted to Presbyterianism, an extreme form of Protestantism. Mary had been brought up as a devout Catholic. There was almost bound to be trouble.

In 1565 Mary decided to marry Henry Stuart, Lord Darnley. He was an English subject, despite the fact that he was Scottish, and a direct descendant – like Mary – of Margaret Tudor, through her second husband the Earl of Angus. Elizabeth did not approve of the marriage, which was not a success in any case. Mary did not give her husband any share in government, preferring instead to confide in her Italian musician, David Riccio. Darnley plotted with the Protestant Scottish lords, and in March 1566 Riccio was dragged from the Queen's presence and murdered. In June that year Mary gave birth to a son, the future James VI of Scotland and James I of England.

Opposite Mary Queen of Scots in 1578, after ten years of captivity in England. Notice the crucifix pendant she is wearing.

"And David was thrown down the stairs from the palace where he was slain, and brought to the Porter's lodge, who taking off his clothes said, 'this was his destiny; for upon this chest was his first bed when he came to this place, and now he lieth a very niggard and misknown knave.' The King's dagger was found sticking in his side. The Queen enquired at the King where his dagger was. [*Darnley*] answered that he wist not well. 'Well,' said the Queen, 'it will be known hereafter.'" *Lord Ruthven's description of the murder of Riccio, favourite of Mary Queen of Scots.*

Darnley's place in Mary's life had meanwhile been taken by James Hepburn, Earl of Bothwell. In February 1567, Darnley was sleeping in a house at Kirk o' Field near Edinburgh, while recovering from an illness. During the night of the 9th, the house was blown up, and Darnley's body was discovered in the garden. It was obvious that he had not died as a result of the explosion, but had been murdered either before or after the event. Rumours were rife; everyone knew that Mary and Darnley had been at loggerheads. It seemed clear that Bothwell was implicated in the murder, perhaps with Mary's consent. A fortnight later Elizabeth wrote to Mary with unusual frankness and warned her of the danger she was in.

Mary chose to ignore these warnings from Elizabeth. In May, Bothwell divorced his wife, and a week later he married the Queen. This provoked the Scottish lords to rebel again. Mary was imprisoned in Loch Leven Castle, and on 24th July she abdicated in favour of her baby son. In May, 1568, she escaped, met with an army provided by her friends, and tried to win back her throne, but was defeated and fled to England. From that moment until she died almost twenty years later, she was a constant thorn in the flesh for Elizabeth. She

A medal bearing a portrait of Mary Queen of Scots, made in Italy in 1572.

was a queen in her own right, with a strong claim to the throne of England. Moreover she was a Catholic, and the focus for all the discontented Catholics who wished to depose Elizabeth.

Chief of these was the Duke of Norfolk, who plotted with Mary and the Earls of Northumberland and Westmorland to proclaim the Queen of Scots as Elizabeth's successor, and bring Catholicism back to England. Mary was also to marry Norfolk. The plot was discovered, and Norfolk was sent to the Tower in 1569. The Earls rebelled rather than go to London and answer charges, but they were easily defeated by the loyal militia. Northumberland was eventually beheaded at York in 1572. Norfolk, meanwhile, had been released in August, 1570, but again started plotting, this time with the Italian banker Ridolfi. Norfolk was condemned to death in January, 1572, though even then Elizabeth was reluctant to let him be executed; only in the face of insistent demands from Parliament did she give way.

It became more and more obvious to Elizabeth that as long as Mary was alive and in captivity on English soil, she would be a cause of unrest. At one stage Elizabeth even thought of restoring Mary to the throne of Scotland, which might at least have taken the unrest elsewhere. The rebellion in the North hardened her views, and the bull *Regnans in excelsis*, pronounced in 1570 by Pope Pius V, only made the situation worse. It instructed the faithful not to obey heretical Protestant rulers, and so it forced Elizabeth's Catholic subjects to choose between loyalty to their Queen or their religion. It was a misconceived and mistimed action of the Pope's, since it encouraged Elizabeth to persecute the Catholics when she would rather have left them alone.

Elizabeth's religious policy did become more rigid and less tolerant – the penalties for failure to attend church services were made more severe – but this was not because her own attitude had hardened. She was forced to take tougher measures as the danger from her enemies grew ever more serious.

Sir Francis Walsingham, Elizabeth's Secretary of State, who was responsible for investigating the conspiracies against her.

"We for our parts utterly deny that either Pope or Cardinal hath power or authority to command or licence any man to consent to mortal sin. Much less can this disloyal, wicked and unnatural purpose by any means be made lawful, to wit, that a native-born subject may seek the effusion of the sacred blood of his anointed sovereign."
Letter to Queen Elizabeth from Sir Thomas Tresham, a Catholic, assuring her of his and other Catholics' loyalty.

6 Proposals of Marriage

Elizabeth enjoyed staghunting (*below*), and falconry (*right*). Two illustrations from Turberville's *Book of Venery* (hunting), published in 1577.

VERY EARLY IN THE REIGN of the Virgin Queen, as she later came to be called, King Eric of Sweden became a suitor for her hand. Elizabeth made it very clear that she would refuse, but early in 1560 Eric determined to set sail for England. Providential storms drove him back, but the marriage problem remained one of crucial importance, for the Queen, for Parliament, and for England. On the one hand, if she did not marry and produce a child, the succession to the throne would cause conflict; on the other, to marry either an English lord or a foreign prince would involve taking sides in her husband's quarrels and so lead to further problems.

In 1570, for example, it was proposed that Elizabeth should marry Henri, Duke of Anjou, younger brother of Charles IX, King of France. Negotiations dragged on for almost two years until Henri – a devout Catholic – demanded total freedom to practise his religion, which Elizabeth could not permit. The Queen Mother of France, Catherine de' Medici, who wanted an ally against Spain, was not to be put off, and next proposed her youngest son, Hercule-François, Duke of Alençon. The massacre of the Protestants on St. Bartholomew's Eve in 1572 halted negotiations for a time, but they began again in 1573.

In May, 1574, Charles IX died, and his brother Henri, Duke of Anjou, became King Henri III of France. There was great rivalry between the last two brothers, King and Duke, and when Elizabeth realized that Henri opposed Alençon's plans to invade the Netherlands, she took his proposals of marriage seriously once more. In 1578 Alençon took the title of Duke of Anjou vacated by his brother. Negotiations

The two paintings *bottom left* and *far left* were made about 1590, the others during the 1570s. Elizabeth obviously approved a style in which she should be painted, and thereafter many artists made her look almost alike. They concentrated on painting the details of her elaborate costumes and jewellery, and on symbols for her purity and virginity: the phoenix (*above far left*), the ermine (*above left*), the rose (*above far right* and *left*), and the pearls that she wears in every picture. To those who saw them, the paintings must have conveyed the artists' idea of perfect beauty rather than the image of a real person.

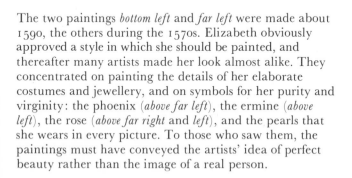

The Earl of Leicester, wearing the thick breeches padded with horse-hair which were fashionable at this time.

lingered on until his death in 1584. By this time, Elizabeth's child-bearing days were over, and Mary Queen of Scots or else her son James had become the natural successor. For Elizabeth, it was more important to keep the Netherlands ports out of the hands of the French (and if possible the Spanish too), than to make a hasty marriage.

The marriage question, and (even more worryingly for the nation) the succession question, were areas in which Elizabeth resented interference, from Parliament or even from trusted friends and counsellors. It is hard to say what her innermost feelings were in the matter. Did she have some physical disability which meant that she could never bear children? She was certainly aware of the natural appetites, however, having been plunged into awareness at an early age when living with Catherine Parr. It seems certain that she loved Robert Dudley, Earl of Leicester. Indeed, when she was ill with smallpox in 1562 and thought that she was going to die, she is said to have sworn that although she "loved Lord Robert dearly, as God was her witness, nothing improper had ever passed between them."

Elizabeth was extremely conscious of her position as Queen, however, and all too aware of the problems Mary Queen of Scots had created for herself in marrying beneath her. Sir Robert Naunton said that Elizabeth once put Leicester in his place with the words: "God's death! My Lord, I will have here but one mistress and no master." Another and much more powerful obstacle to their marriage was the fact that in September, 1560, Leicester's wife Amy Robsart was found dead at the bottom of a flight of stairs in suspicious circumstances. After that, if Elizabeth had married Leicester, people might have said that she was an accomplice to a murder.

Elizabeth's affection for Leicester found its counterpart at the end of her life in her affection – or infatuation – for the Earl of Essex. She may also have been wanting to relive her younger days, and recapture the vitality of Leicester, but the problem created by the

Elizabeth dances with the Earl of
Leicester while other courtiers look
on in admiration.

difference in their ranks was still there. It was much
easier for a king to marry a subject and make her his
consort than it was for a reigning queen to do likewise.

On the other hand, any alliance with a foreign prince
was bound to have serious consequences for England
in the shifting balance of power in Europe. After her
illness of October, 1562, the Commons petitioned
Elizabeth to marry. Her reply was characteristic:
"Though after my death you may have many step-
dames, yet shall you never have a more natural mother
than I mean to be."

She thought of herself as the daughter, bride and
mother of England, and in this approach to her position
as Queen and to her life as a whole, there was under-
standably little room for a husband.

7 The Dutch Revolt

ELIZABETH TRIED TO KEEP OUT of European conflicts, but events in the Netherlands seemed bound to involve England sooner or later. After France, the Netherlands were the nearest part of mainland Europe. In times of oppression Englishmen had fled there, and Dutch people had often been welcomed in England. Antwerp was a major port, which had close commercial links with London as well as competing with it for overseas trade. When the southern Netherlands had formed part of the Duchy of Burgundy, an English princess had married into the ruling house.

The area which is now Holland and Belgium, with a small part of northern France, had come under Spanish rule through dynastic marriage. Since the Reformation, the Dutch had been converted to Protestantism, and the Flemish people in the south had remained loyal to their Catholic faith. In both areas the Spanish rulers were hated by the people. Three leaders emerged on the Netherlands side – Counts Egmont and Hoorn, and Prince William of Orange – who, despite their moderation, were unable to prevent the outbreak of violent protest. In 1566 the Dutch revolted, and, especially in Antwerp, there was a wild outburst of Protestant iconoclasm (the damaging of religious paintings and other church adornments).

Philip II of Spain sent the Duke of Alva to put down the revolt, which he did, with extreme cruelty, the following year. Egmont and Hoorn were executed, and Orange fled. Alva's victory seemed complete, when in 1572 Elizabeth decided to expel from English ports a band of Dutch pirates known as the Sea Beggars. They

Opposite Sir Francis Drake in 1580, shortly after his return from sailing round the world.

Elizabeth, accompanied by Lord Burghley, receives ambassadors from the Dutch rebels, who were asking for her help against Spain.

had been preying on Spanish shipping – along with Elizabeth's own "sea dogs", including Drake and Hawkins – and obviously were something of an embarrassment to her. Even so, it was hard to see exactly what her motive was, since she was under no pressure from Spain at the time. In the event her action did much to improve relations with Spain, and the following year trade between the two countries was resumed. This was important for England, since she was becoming more dependent on trade for her prosperity, and the great influx of gold and silver from South America had made Spain the richest country in Europe.

The other result of Elizabeth's action was much more far reaching. The expelled Sea Beggars went home to their native country and captured the port of Brill in southern Holland. They then seized nearby Flushing, Middelburg and Zierikzee, and controlled the whole Scheldt estuary and the approaches to Antwerp, both the centre of Spanish government and the largest trading centre in the world at that time. The Duke of Alva retaliated by laying siege to Haarlem; but most of Holland and Zeeland was liberated.

In 1577 Alexander Farnese, Prince of Parma, re-

"Her Majesty, I see, my lord, oftentimes doth fall into mislike of this cause [*intervention in the Netherlands*] but I trust that, seeing that mine and other men's poor lives and substances are adventured for her sake . . . she will fortify and maintain her own action to the full performance of that she hath agreed on."
The Earl of Leicester writing to Lord Burghley.

placed Alva as Governor of the Netherlands. Elizabeth was giving support to the Protestants, and the Catholics appealed to the Duke of Alençon (later Anjou) for his help. In August, 1580, Anjou was invited to become King of the United Provinces. Elizabeth was not at all pleased with the idea, particularly as she was then in the middle of marriage negotiations with him. His death in 1584 was, from this point of view, very fortunate, but the assassination of William of Orange in the same year threw the United Provinces into disorder once more.

Elizabeth, who also had been invited by the rebels to become ruler of the United Provinces, decided to take action. In August, 1585, she made a treaty with the Dutch and promised them soldiers and money. The Earl of Leicester was sent over as commander, and arrived there in December. On 1st January, 1586, he was offered the absolute governorship, which he accepted some three weeks later, much to Elizabeth's fury. He had not told her of the invitation, nor asked her permission to accept it. Elizabeth's anger was increased because it was widely said that he and his wife were to set up a court to rival her own. Her letter to Leicester left him in little doubt as to her feelings: "How contemptuously we conceive ourself to have been used by you, you shall by this bearer (her emissary) understand. . . . We could never have imagined had we not seen it fall out in experience that a man raised up by ourself and extraordinarily favoured by us above any other subject of this land, would have in so contemptible a sort broken our commandment. . . ." In less than six months, however, he had been totally forgiven: ". . . with my million and legion of thanks for all your pains and cares. As you know, ever the same. E.R."

In fact Elizabeth was becoming tired of the drain on her resources, and the following year was looking for a way of getting out of the Netherlands. Sluys was lost in 1587, and 1588 was to bring the Spanish Armada.

In the meantime, the drama of Mary Queen of Scots was reaching its climax.

"Sir, the grief I have taken for the loss of my dear son and yours would not suffer me to write sooner. . . . For my own part, I have lost, beside the comfort of my life, a most principal stay and help in my service here and, if I may say it, I think none of all hath a greater loss than the Queen's Majesty herself." *Leicester to Sir Francis Walsingham on the death of Sir Philip Sidney.*

"For my own part, I will not endure such another year's service, with so many crosses and wants and so little assistance every way, if I were sure to gain as much as all these provinces were worth." *Leicester to Walsingham in the winter of 1586–87, in Holland.*

8 Death of a Queen

MARY QUEEN OF SCOTS had been a prisoner in England since 1568. Her presence was a constant reminder to Elizabeth of what might have happened to herself. Mary was a queen, with a very good claim to the throne of England. She was a woman, too, with an unfortunate love life behind her. This explains much of Elizabeth's treatment of Mary. She sympathized with her as a queen and as a woman, and yet she knew in her heart that Mary was a constant threat to her. So long as the heir presumptive to the throne was a Catholic, there would be a good reason for Elizabeth's Catholic subjects to rebel, especially now they were being encouraged by Jesuit missionaries from the Continent. Elizabeth always refused to see Mary, fearing, no doubt, that her firmness would weaken, and she would show her sympathy. It would have made matters easy for Elizabeth if some loyal subject had assassinated Mary, but in the end the fateful decision was left to her and to her alone.

The crisis came in 1586. Anthony Babington, a Catholic, led a plot to murder Elizabeth and put Mary on the throne. Sir Francis Walsingham, the Secretary of State, had managed to get one of his spies involved in the conspiracy, so he could keep watch on their plans and see their correspondence with Mary. When the time was right he struck, and the conspirators were arrested. They confessed their crime, were tried and executed. Mary's papers were confiscated and searched, and it was established that she had given her consent to the plot. This gave those who had been clamouring for her execution all the ammunition they

"Sir, as I came from London homeward in my coach, I saw at every town's end the number of ten or twelve standing with long staves, and until I came to Enfield I thought no other of them but that they had stayed for avoiding of the rain. But at Enfield . . . when there was no rain, I bethought myself that they were appointed for the apprehending of such as are missing. And thereupon I called some of them to me apart and asked them wherefore they stood there. And one of them answered, 'To take three young men.' And demanding how they should know the persons, one answered with these words, 'Marry, my lord, by intelligence of their favour.' 'What mean you by that?' quoth I. 'Marry,' said they, 'one of the parties hath a hooked nose.'" *Letter from Burghley to Walsingham in August 1586, when the members of the Babington conspiracy were still at large.*

needed. A commission met at Fotheringay to try her, then it moved to Westminster, and pronounced her guilty. Parliament petitioned Elizabeth to have Mary executed. She refused and, as usual, stalled for time, but in December the death sentence was finally pronounced.

Elizabeth and Sir Francis Walsingham identifying the Babington plotters – one of the many nineteenth-century romantic paintings inspired by the story of Mary Queen of Scots.

The trial of Mary Queen of Scots at Fotheringay Castle. Mary is sitting on the right, surrounded by the conspirators.

> "Then one of the executioners, pulling off her garters, espied her little dog which was crept under her clothes, which could not be gotten forth but by force, yet afterward would not depart from the dead corpse, but came and lay between her head and her shoulders, which being imbrued with her blood was carried away and washed."
>
> *Report of the execution of Mary Queen of Scots sent to Burghley.*

Mary's condemnation caused great upsurges of feeling in both France and Scotland. Henri III of France tried to intervene, and naturally James VI of Scotland, Mary's son, remonstrated with Elizabeth. He sent commissioners to talk to Elizabeth about his mother and about the succession question. A letter Elizabeth wrote to him in January, 1587, puts the whole matter in a nutshell. "By saving of her life they would have had mine. Do I not make myself, trow ye, a goodly prey for every wretch to devour? Transfigure yourself into my state, and suppose what you ought to do, and thereafter weigh my life, and reject the care of murder. . . ." James himself, of course, might have become a focus for plots against Elizabeth once his mother was dead, but the Scottish lords had brought him up as a Protestant, so the Queen felt no fear of him.

It was proposed that Mary should be put in the hands of a neutral ruler, but Elizabeth had little faith in such a remedy. People in England now knew that Spain was preparing for war, and Elizabeth came under great pressure from her advisers and from Parliament to sign the death warrant. She did so, but was reluctant to give orders for it to be sent. Lord Burghley, the Lord Treasurer, then asked those members of the Privy Council who agreed with him that Mary must die, to take the responsibility upon themselves. The order reached Fotheringhay on 5th February, and Mary was executed on the 8th. Elizabeth was shocked and horrified when the news reached her, and sent her secretary, Davison, to the Tower.

Elizabeth has often been accused of hypocrisy in the whole affair. Indeed, the letter she sent to James VI after hearing of Mary's execution can certainly be read in this light. On the other hand, she was usually merciful, and the realization that she had killed a fellow monarch must have come as a great shock to her. She knew that the execution would bring upon her the hatred of all the Catholic monarchs of Europe, and lead to reprisals. In this respect the Council acted hastily. Mary would probably not have out-lived Elizabeth,

The execution of Mary Queen of Scots.

and a long war with Spain might well have been avoided.

With Mary dead, Philip of Spain could no longer hope to win England back for Catholicism simply by plotting to overthrow Elizabeth. War thus became inevitable, and the Queen was obliged to try and heal the breach with Scotland. The Spaniards had been making overtures to James VI; and Elizabeth had to be sure of his support if Spain attacked. The tone of her relations with him was often one of exasperation. James was almost certain to be her heir, and yet his behaviour was hardly that of the sort of successor she wanted to see on her throne. When James and his wife quarrelled about the upbringing of their son Henry, the future Prince of Wales, Elizabeth let them know what she thought. When James fled in the face of rebellion by some of his lords, she reproached him for unkingly behaviour. In the end, however, she had to acknowledge that he was the heir to her kingdom.

"I have seen such evident shows of your contrarious dealings . . . and if you suppose that princes' causes be veiled so covertly that no intelligence may betray them, deceive not yourself: we old foxes can find shifts to save ourselves by others' malice, and come by knowledge of greatest secret, specially if it touch our freehold." *Queen Elizabeth to James VI of Scotland.*

9 The Great Armada

IN THE SUMMER OF 1588 the Spanish Armada, long expected by the English, set sail from its anchorage near Lisbon. On 19th July, Captain Thomas Fleming sailed into Plymouth to say that the great armed fleet had been sighted off Land's End. The news was rushed to Elizabeth and her Council in London.

Elizabeth had known since December, 1585, that Philip II of Spain had an invasion of England in mind, but not until the summer of 1586 had she begun to make plans for defence. She ordered her Lords Lieutenant in the counties to muster the militia, or home guard, and to organize a chain of beacons that would stretch along the coast from headland to headland and give warning of enemy ships. But the militia alone could not prevent the landing of a vast army such as the Duke of Parma had ready in the Netherlands, waiting to be picked up by the Armada.

The Navy had to be prepared to take on the Armada at sea and destroy it before it reached England. The naval captains, under Sir John Hawkins, were eager to fight, and confident in the superiority of their ships, which were smaller but speedier and better-armed than the Spanish galleons. But it was impossibly expensive to keep the Navy on a war footing all the time. New ships were built and old ones repaired, but the fleet lay idle at Plymouth and in the Thames Estuary while the Spanish preparations went ahead.

In the spring of 1587 Elizabeth gave way a little and agreed to let Sir Francis Drake take four of her ships along with sixteen privately-owned ones on a raid to Cadiz – an action which has since been known as the

Sir John Hawkins, sailor and explorer knighted for his part in the defeat of the Armada.

Singeing of the King of Spain's Beard. Many of the ships at anchor in Cadiz harbour, where they had been gathered in readiness for the invasion of England, were sunk, and others were badly damaged. A raid on Lisbon was also planned, but it would have been extremely dangerous; instead Drake captured a Portuguese galleon off the Azores, carrying treasure worth about £140,000. The raid on Cadiz certainly achieved its aim – to delay the date of the Armada's sailing – and Elizabeth received £40,000 as her share of the captured treasure. Elizabeth's sea-captains liked this policy of lightning raids, which allowed them to win money and fame, but the Queen herself was less pleased. She saw the navy as an arm of defence to stop an army crossing the Channel, rather than as an attacking force; she probably still hoped to talk her way to peace with Spain. In the last resort she held the whip hand, because by keeping the navy short of food, ammunition and other supplies she made sure it was unable to put to sea. Throughout the late summer and autumn of 1587 rumour was rife that the great Armada had set sail, and the English fleet took its position in the Channel. By January of 1588 it was obvious that there would not be any attack until the late spring at the earliest, so Elizabeth cut the active strength of the fleet by half.

1588 had been declared a fateful year by many astrologers and soothsayers. Philip Melancthon, one of the leading scholars of the German reformation, had calculated that the final historical cycle since the birth of Jesus Christ would end in that year, and that the Day of Judgment was at hand. For the Queen herself, the eclipse of the moon that year coincided with the beginning of her own ruling sign of Virgo.

Undaunted, Elizabeth continued to make her plans. Lord Howard of Effingham was put in command of the navy, with Henry Seymour (based on Dover) and Francis Drake (based on Plymouth) under him. Elizabeth demanded a forced loan from those of her subjects able to pay, and raised £75,000, though it took

A dockyard blacksmith making equipment for the English fleet.

43

Below left Two stages in the battle of the Armada – the English fleet makes contact with the Spaniards off Portland Bill, and then harasses it along the channel.
Below right The wind appears to take the side of the English as the damaged Spanish fleet leaves Calais, while armed men guard the Essex coast.
On following pages The Armada (right) kept closely to its disciplined sailing pattern throughout the battle, but the smaller, more mobile British ships were able to make repeated attacks.

some time to collect. Luckily, Parliament was not in session at the time, for in spite of Elizabeth's skill in handling the members, they might well have insisted on concessions in other areas, such as toleration for the Puritans, before agreeing to such heavy taxation. As it was, they agreed that her emergency measures were needed. Even the notorious ship money, a tax levied in the seaboard counties and coastal towns to help pay for the navy, was regarded as justifiable. Elizabeth's own money reserve had shrunk from almost £300,000 to about £55,000, and even this was worth less and less as the flood of American gold and silver caused prices to rise all over Europe.

The Spanish Armada, under the Duke of Medina Sidonia, left Lisbon in May, to pick up its invasion army in the Netherlands, but it was damaged by gales, and put into harbours along the Bay of Biscay to refit. Lord

Howard set off to attack them, but the wind veered to the south, so he sailed on to Plymouth, realizing that the same wind would bring the Spaniards to England. On 21st July he sailed out of Plymouth to meet the Armada, and for more than a week a running fight took place up the Channel. When the great Spanish fleet reached Calais it had scarcely been harmed, but Howard sent in eight fire ships, blazing hulks which drifted in amongst the anchored Spanish fleet and caused panic, and a great deal of damage. The next day – 29th July – the battle proper began. The Spanish were already confused and demoralized, and the English won a surprisingly easy victory. Those Spanish ships that were not sunk in the fighting or forced ashore, were driven by gales into the North Sea and eventually around the coasts of Scotland and Ireland. Many were wrecked, and only a few survived to reach Cadiz.

"This noon there comes from Holland a vessel which was at Enkhuizen actually on the last day of July. It brings news that eighteen ships of the Spanish Armada were sunk by gunfire, and eight taken and brought to England. The rest of the Spanish Armada has fled to the French coast. If this is true it will somewhat abate Spanish insolence and give the English fresh courage, though they have no lack of insolence either."
Letter from Hans Buttber to the Fugger Bank of Augsburg, which was owed a large amount of money by Philip II of Spain, 3rd August, 1588.

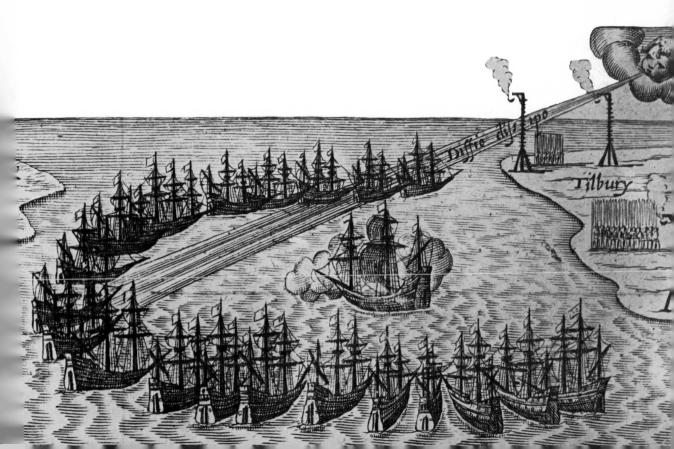

Meanwhile Elizabeth decided to go to Tilbury, on the Thames estuary, where her army had been assembled in case the Spaniards had managed to land. Her speech to the men on that occasion was one of her most characteristic and most justly famous. For her, the defeat of Spain proved the value of everything she had tried to do for England. The war went on until after Elizabeth's death, but the threat to England's island security was not repeated. The mighty power of Spain, which for years had seemed invincible, had at last been checked, and soon began to decline. This great victory was crucial for England's survival as an independent Protestant country.

Elizabeth celebrated her own part in the achievement by having two medals struck – one in 1588 and the other in 1589 – and a special portrait painted (*back cover*). She was indeed *Eliza triumphans*.

"Therefore I am come amongst you, as you see, at this time, not for my recreation and disport, but being resolved, in the midst and heat of the battle, to live or die amongst you all, to lay down for my God, and for my kingdom, and for my people, my honour and my blood, even in the dust. I know I have the body of a weak and feeble woman, but I have the heart and stomach of a king, and of a king of England, too."
Queen Elizabeth's speech to the army at Tilbury, 8th August, 1588.

10 Catholics and Puritans

ELIZABETH'S TRIUMPH OVER THE ARMADA overshadowed another triumph, the success of her religious settlement. Even if it never reconciled the Puritans to the Church of England, at least it avoided the long and bitter conflicts that were going on in France and the Netherlands. The years 1588 and 1589 saw the publication of a series of Puritan pamphlets known as the Marprelate Tracts, which attacked episcopacy (the control of the Church by bishops) in the Church of England. Their offensive and slanderous nature lost the Puritans a good deal of public sympathy, and John Whitgift, Archbishop of Canterbury, was determined to bring the authors to heel.

Elizabeth's three successive Archbishops of Canterbury give some clues as to how religious affairs progressed during her reign. Her first was the scholarly Matthew Parker (1504–75). A moderate reformer under Henry VIII, he himself took advantage of permission for the clergy to marry under Edward VI (1548). Parker was Master of Corpus Christi College, Cambridge, until 1553. When Mary came to the throne, he wisely disappeared from view, until in 1559 Elizabeth chose him as her Archbishop of Canterbury. She never quite came to terms with his marriage, however, and on leaving the Archbishop's house after being entertained there, said to his wife: "Madam I may not call you; mistress I am ashamed to call you; but however, I thank you."

Despite his moderate policies, Matthew Parker aroused Puritan opposition, voiced in the *Admonition of Parliament*, a pamphlet published in 1572. The contro-

Opposite left The Armada did not in fact approach as close as this to the English coast, but the picture shows preparations for its arrival: rowing-boats to warn of its arrival, beacons to spread the message, and cannon and pikemen to defend the shore.
Opposite right Elizabeth goes to St Paul's Cathedral to give thanks for England's escape from the Spanish menace.

Above Elizabeth's three Archbishops of Canterbury. Left to right, Matthew Parker (1559–75), Edmund Grindal (1575–83) and John Whitgift (1583–1604).
Opposite Hatred between Protestants and Catholics throughout Europe increased after the Massacre of St Bartholomew, in 1572, when about fifteen thousand French Protestants were murdered by order of the King's mother, Catherine de' Medici.

"A very strange thing sure it were, that such a discipline as ye [*the Puritans*] speak of should be taught by Christ and his apostles in the word of God, and no church ever have found it out, nor received it till this present time." *Richard Hooker, Ecclesiastical Polity, a book which set out to explain and justify the doctrine and institutions of the Church of England.*

versy it stirred up inspired the theologian Richard Hooker to write his *Ecclesiastical Polity*, an exposition of the beliefs and organization of the Church of England. In the *Second Admonition to Parliament*, the Puritans complained about the exiles who had left the country during Mary's reign and returned when Elizabeth came to the Throne. "What talk they of their being beyond the seas in Queen Mary's days because of the persecution, when they in Queen Elizabeth's days, are come home to raise a persecution?" Many people found their loyalties divided by the religious issues. The experience of exile and persecution had left Puritans and Churchmen alike bitter and unwilling to compromise. Although in face of the Spanish threat they had good reasons for settling their quarrels, in fact the atmosphere of hostility grew steadily worse.

In many respects the Puritans were the most dangerous opponents of the Church of England, since there were many rich and powerful men among them. Also their opposition was born of theological belief, while those who wanted a return to Rome did so very much for nostalgic reasons. The disaster of the official

Catholic and Protestant religious propaganda. *Right* Edmund Campion, a Jesuit who was executed in 1581 for trying to revive English Catholicism; in the background are scenes from the tortures which he was said to have suffered.

Far right According to the Protestant version, William Parry was given absolution in advance by the Pope for killing Queen Elizabeth, but was put off simply by her commanding presence.

return to Catholic worship under Queen Mary, and the aggression of Spain, had further weakened the position of the English Catholics. Many people were happy to conform even though they kept in their hearts a secret preference for the old religion.

Edmund Grindal, Elizabeth's second Archbishop of Canterbury from 1575, had definite Puritan leanings. Under Queen Mary he had taken refuge in Frankfurt in Germany; and had tried to heal some of the more

Deus Vindex

bitter disputes which split the Protestant refugees there. In 1559 he was made Bishop of London. In 1577, Elizabeth instructed him to suppress "prophesyings", secret Puritan gatherings for prayer and preaching which were often conducted by Church of England ministers, and which threatened to replace the Prayer Book services in some parts of the country. He refused, was suspended from his functions until 1582, and died in 1583. Elizabeth would see to it that such a thing could not happen again.

John Whitgift, who succeeded Grindal, was a much more convinced upholder of the Church of England than either of his two predecessors. Although a Calvinist by belief, he upheld the vision of a Church that was firmly neither Roman Catholic nor Puritan. In 1586 Elizabeth made him a member of her Council – the first bishop to achieve that position. Whitgift was determined that the Church of England, which had begun life as a politically motivated compromise, should develop a distinct theology of its own. He rejected the Catholic idea that only through the Church could a Christian gain salvation, but even so he regarded organization as being almost as important as faith. The Queen herself had always kept her personal beliefs in subjection to the demands of the day. During her brother Edward's reign she had been thought of as something of a Puritan, though her taste in furnishings for her private chapel in her own reign was markedly more Catholic. Her "public" religion was somewhere between the two. When she was asked whether the bread and wine of the Communion service really became the body and blood of Jesus Christ (a fruitful source of religious argument in the sixteenth century), she gave a typically enigmatic answer:

> "'Twas God the word that spake it,
> He took the Bread and brake it;
> And what the word did make it;
> That I believe, and take it."

Elizabeth disliked Puritanism as she disliked Roman Catholicism: both attacked her personal authority. In the later years of her reign both came under attack from Archbishop Whitgift. In her personal faith she liked a more Lutheran form of worship, and the Lutheran view that the ruler should determine the religion of the country naturally suited her, too. Not all Puritans were critical of the Queen, by any means. Edmund Spenser, who devoted his poetic skill to glorifying her reign, and Sir Philip Sidney, who died in her service, were both Puritans. In 1579 John Stubbes had his right hand cut off for writing a pamphlet against Elizabeth's proposed marriage to the Duke of Alençon, but he was such a loyal subject that he took off his hat with his left hand and shouted "God Save the Queen!" before he fainted.

And so Puritan opposition in Parliament was all the harder for Elizabeth to deal with. The Puritans were her loyal subjects, in fact some of her most loyal. She needed them, and the country needed them. To have given them all they asked would have been to make the country ungovernable, since they could not agree among themselves, and other sections of the nation would have been diametrically opposed, as they were to be some fifty years later. As for the Catholics, it was not their beliefs which made them enemies of the Queen. Early in the reign, they too had displayed great loyalty. After 1570, when the Papal Bull *Regnans in excelsis* instructed Catholics to overthrow heretic rulers, they became a serious threat, especially in view of the military danger from Catholic Spain. Even so, it was only the foreign-trained Jesuits who suffered death for their beliefs: Whitgift's persecution of native Puritans and Catholics was very mild by the standards of the time.

Sir Philip Sidney, poet and soldier, who died in 1586 fighting the Spanish in the Netherlands, painted by Nicholas Hilliard in the typical pose of a rejected lover.

HONI SOIT QVI MAL Y PENSE

The most noble ROBERT
Earle of Essex and Ewe, Earle
Marshall of England, Vicount He:
reford and Bourgcher, Lord Ferres
of Chartley, L. Bourgcher and
Louayn, and her Maiesties
lieutenant, and Gouernour generall
of the Kingdome of Irland. 1601.

11 Elizabeth and Essex

THE DEFEAT OF THE ARMADA was the peak of Elizabeth's achievement. In the years that followed, a series of problems in her personal life meant that she was unable to enjoy the fruits of her triumph to the full. Within a week of victory her friend of thirty years' standing, the Earl of Leicester, was dead. The relationship had had its difficult moments, and there were times when they infuriated each other. Leicester's last letter was one of the few particularly precious items Elizabeth kept in a box by her bed, and in her own hand were written the words: "His last letter."

Elizabeth was now over fifty-five, and in her deepening loneliness she found solace in the company of Leicester's stepson, Robert Devereux, Earl of Essex. In April, 1589, Francis Drake and John Norris took an expedition to Portugal to help the pretender Don Antonio recover his country, which had been ruled by Spain since 1580. Essex was now twenty-one, and against Elizabeth's orders he slipped away and joined the expedition. Elizabeth was furious, and summoned him home at once. But her letter took six weeks to reach him – he received it on his return, in fact – by which time he was forgiven.

This type of incident was to be repeated throughout the relationship between the ageing monarch and the young hero. When Elizabeth sent troops to France in 1591 to help Henri of Navarre, the Protestant heir to the throne, against the Catholic League supported by Spain, Essex took command of the force in Normandy. Elizabeth had to rebuke Essex more than once for his rashness, and it seemed obvious that he was bent on

"Her Majesty seemed to all to shine through courtesy: but as she was not easy to receive any to especial grace, so she was most constant to those whom she received, and of great judgement to know to what point of greatness men were fit to be advanced." *Sir John Hayward (1564?–1627), The Annals of Queen Elizabeth.*

Opposite Robert Devereux, Earl of Essex, drawn in 1601, just before his downfall.

winning a reputation for bravery rather than strategy.

Spanish aggression continued, largely because Philip II saw himself as the defender of the Catholic Church throughout Europe. He seemed not to have taken to heart the lesson of the 1588 Armada as far as England was concerned. In late 1595 and early 1596 a combined naval and military attack against Spain was organized, but Elizabeth delayed giving the commission to Essex – with Howard as Lord Admiral – until the very last moment, when the Spaniards were attacking Calais. The town fell to the attackers, and so the English expedition spent the next six weeks preparing itself for an attack on Cadiz. This was extremely profitable, but had no effect on the course of the war. Another expedition was planned to attack Spain the following year, but bad weather held it back at the most opportune

moment, and it sailed for the Azores in the hopes of finding a Spanish treasure fleet. This time Essex was away for nearly two months, and on his return found the country worried about a possible attack by a new Spanish Armada. Elizabeth was certainly glad to have him back, since troubles in Ireland were causing her alarm, and she badly needed someone of Essex's calibre to take control of the situation.

Hugh O'Neill, Earl of Tyrone, had been in open rebellion since 1596, with the support of most of the Catholic population. England's control over Ireland had never been very secure, and now the religious divisions had made matters worse, while Elizabeth's policy of "planting" English Protestant settlers had roused the anger of the displaced Irish. Essex was highly critical of the way matters were being handled, and in late 1598 he was made Lord Deputy. The following March he set out with 16,000 men to take up his command. He was, however, no more successful than his predecessors. Elizabeth wrote bitter letters complaining of his failure to do the job, and of the fortune she was having to spend on subduing the Irish. Finally Essex decided to attack the rebel Tyrone, but by this time his army was reduced to a quarter of its original size. At the council of war held in Dublin, all the commanders opposed his scheme. Essex made them sign a paper to this effect and sent it to Elizabeth, then decided to attack Tyrone all the same. In fact he met Tyrone and, recognizing the hopelessness of the position, agreed to a truce on 6th September. Three weeks later he suddenly appeared back in England at Nonsuch Palace, near Epsom, and burst into the Queen's presence before she was even dressed. Ignoring her command not to leave his post, he had come to justify his actions.

Defeat in Ireland – at least as far as his ambitions were concerned – merely spurred Essex on the more. It seemed as if a head-on collision with Elizabeth was now inevitable. She could have sent him to the Tower, but instead she placed him in the custody of the Lord Keeper at York House. Essex was not sent for trial

Above Irish Catholics were accused of many atrocities, including forcing women and children to drown.

Opposite Festivities on the lake at Elvetham, Hampshire, in 1591, in honour of Elizabeth's visit.

before the Star Chamber, but was later confined at the Queen's pleasure in Essex House, and prevented from acting in any of his official capacities. He was always short of money, and when Elizabeth refused to renew his monopoly on the trade in sweet wines – his chief source of income – he retorted angrily that her "conditions were as crooked as her carcase."

Essex then formed a desperate plot to capture the Tower, the City of London and the Court at Whitehall, and make Elizabeth his prisoner so that she would declare him Lord Protector. To set the mood of the times and make his intentions clear, he bribed the players at the Globe Theatre to perform Shakespeare's *Richard II* – which justifies rebellion against a bad king – on 7th February. This time he had gone too far for Elizabeth to tolerate, and she summoned him to court to explain himself. When he failed to appear she sent the Lord Keeper to fetch him. Essex took the Lord Keeper and his men prisoners, and in so doing sealed his own fate. He was declared a traitor, and was executed privately inside the Tower on Ash Wednesday, 1601.

The war in Ireland was to continue for the rest of Elizabeth's reign – in fact in 1601 a Spanish army landed at Kinsale, on the south coast, but it was too small to tip the scales – but Lord Mountjoy, who followed Essex, slowly broke the power of Tyrone and the other rebels.

12 Power and Poverty

ONE OF THE COMMONEST IMAGES of Elizabeth's England is that of the magnificent Queen surrounded by her daring sea-captains. She is shown as such in a Victorian stained-glass window in St. Margaret's Church, Westminster. The exploits of Sir Francis Drake, Sir John Hawkins and others, in war and in exploration, produced a feeling of national greatness; and William Shakespeare, Christopher Marlowe, Ben Jonson and many lesser-known poets and playwrights gave England a culture which rivalled those of France and Italy. This sense of achievement, much of it under Elizabeth's patronage, together with her own personal splendour, has given the age a golden glow in the eyes of later generations. This period, freed from the shackles of medieval feudalism and Catholicism, and managing to postpone the bitter conflicts of the following century, must truly have been the age of Merrie England.

There is certainly much to justify this impression. It was a time of great flamboyance in dress and behaviour, though our modern view of this is too much based on what we know of London and the Court. For the peasants, who made up most of the population, life was still hard and there was no money to spare for luxuries. For most of the reign the harvests were good and food prices low – in the 1590s, when the economic situation worsened, discontent grew at all levels of society.

England was in fact experiencing the Renaissance, or process of cultural rebirth, which had begun in Italy during the fifteenth century. This was an escape from the traditional ways of thinking, determined by the power of the Catholic Church and by the feudal system

Below Elizabeth painted by Marcus Gheeraerts in one of the most elaborate of all her dresses, covered in pearls and decorated with pears, grapes, pomegranates, lilies and roses.

61

POLY-OLBION

By
Michaell Drayton,
Esqr:

London printed for { M. Lownes. I. Browne. Cnotanz
I. Helme. I. Busbie. [...] W. [...]

Opposite George Clifford, Earl of Cumberland, the Queen's Champion at her Accession Day tournament, in his costume as Knight of Pendragon Castle. The customs of courtly chivalry were revived, and knights and ladies played characters from Arthurian legends.
Left The frontispiece of Michael Drayton's poem *Poly-olbion* shows Britannia wearing a map of the flourishing English countryside and holding a *cornucopia*, a symbol of Britain's prosperity and fruitfulness.

of land-holding, both of which had made each individual seem much less important than the society to which he belonged. The Renaissance came late to England, but it came at a time when there was a generous supply of talent in the arts, in statecraft and in military leadership, coupled with a sudden realization of national identity. Elizabeth gave the country a chance to develop this new sense of purpose; for much of the reign she gave England peace and prosperity, and an atmosphere in which the new spirit of the age could flourish. She personified those forces that were holding the nation together, when religious and social conflicts threatened to tear it apart.

Naturally, not all the episodes of her reign were glorious, either in terms of victory and achievement or of the way people behaved. It was still a barbaric age by modern standards – political rivals were disposed of by assassination, or execution if one controlled the processes of law. There were forces at work, too, which even the best-informed statesmen and financiers could not understand properly – often the same forces, such as inflation and unemployment, which politicians still misjudge today. The flood of seemingly unlimited Spanish gold from America ought, so people thought, to have been a great blessing, but all it did was to cause prices to rise and make the poor even poorer. It was not

A nobleman throws a coin to a beggar but disdains to look at him. Notice the bandage round his leg – many beggars feigned injury or disease to attract more sympathy.

64

yet understood that money only derived its value from the production of goods; windfall profits were still spent on luxury consumption when they should have been invested in new industries. Inflation was not seen for what it was until too late. The new Poor Law of 1601 was passed, and the system of selling monopolies in various trades was abandoned. Both these measures were meant to reduce the hardship caused by the economic crisis, but Elizabeth and her ministers had no power to create wealth for the nation.

Drake, Hawkins and Raleigh might bring in short-term profits from their buccaneering expeditions, but of much more lasting benefit was the activity of the

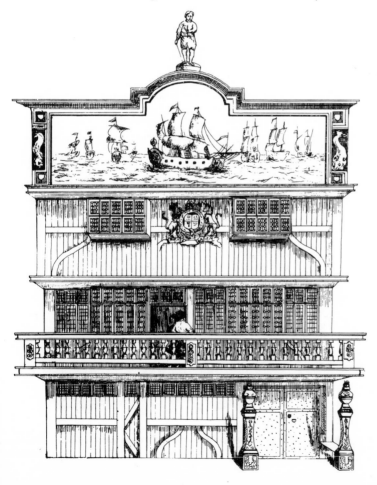

The East India Company was founded in 1600 in this house in Leadenhall Street, City of London.

merchant adventurers, especially the founding of the East India Company in 1600. Trade, rather than family alliances or religious considerations, slowly became the main influence on England's foreign policy. The next reign was to produce the extraordinary sight of the heir to the throne (later Charles I) courting the Spanish Infanta, in spite of the tremendous bitterness between the two peoples.

The Treaty of Blois, signed in 1572, gave Elizabeth her first ally. England and France agreed to help each other if either was attacked, and not to help each other's enemies. The immediate result was that the French stopped interfering in Scotland, and accepted England's dominant position there. In the same year Elizabeth had improved her relations with Spain by driving out the Sea Beggars. As we have seen (page 35), in the long run this was to be a great help for the Dutch rebels, but for the moment it served to give England peace and security. Both events show how Elizabeth's diplomacy was a matter of practical calculation, and had little to do with religious or any other principles.

It is easy to be misled by Elizabeth's triumphant success as Queen and by the long and glorious sequence of English achievements in war and in exploration, into a false sense of her own and her country's importance. England was smaller, weaker and poorer than France and Spain, and Elizabeth's foreign policy always had to be dictated by the way the tide was running on the continent. As long as England seemed threatened by Spain, her main concern was to limit Spanish power in the rest of Europe. Until the defeat of the Armada in 1588 it was always dangerous to give too much help to the Dutch for fear of Spanish reprisals. However sympathetic Elizabeth might have been to the French Protestants, she could not risk meddling too deeply in France's internal politics. Any reduction of the Spanish presence in the Netherlands was desirable from Elizabeth's point of view, but there was little point in simply replacing Spanish strength by French strength.

Vitally governing any decision about military in-

> "I am your anointed queen. I will never be by violence constrained to do anything. I thank God I am endued with such qualities that if I were turned out of the Realm in my petticoat I were able to live in any place in Christome."
> *Queen Elizabeth to Parliament, 1566.*

volvement was the question of finance. In 1588 Elizabeth's total state revenue was about £400,000, of which £120,000 was spent on the army in the Netherlands, and some £150,000 on the fleet. In 1570 she had spent less than £10,000 on the fleet, though by 1586 and 1587 it had passed £30,000 and £40,000 respectively. In the last fifteen years of her reign she gave nearly £1,500,000 in aid to the Dutch, and some £300,000 to Henri of Navarre, the French Protestant leader who became King Henri IV. The cost of the fighting in Ireland amounted to nearly £2,000,000. The time would soon come, however, when the monarch could no longer be expected to finance the country's wars out of the crown's private revenues. Elizabeth repeatedly had to ask her Parliaments to vote subsidies (taxes); and as this became more and more usual, the Members of Parliament demanded an ever-increasing say in why and how the money was spent.

A procession of Knights of the Garter in about 1575. Third from left is Lord Burghley, and second from right Lord Howard of Effingham.

13 Painters, Musicians and Poets

THE REIGN OF ELIZABETH saw a remarkable flowering of artistic talent in England. During the fifteenth century, Italian painters such as Raphael and Botticelli, and sculptors such as Michelangelo, had broken away from the tradition of Gothic religious art. They had looked back to Greek and Roman models, but also forward to give a new freedom to the artist's imagination. This Renaissance, or rebirth of culture, took some time to reach Great Britain. When it arrived it was fostered by the new wealth arising from trade and from the dissolution of the monasteries, and by the death of the feudal system, which led to the concentration of rich educated men at court in London.

Decorative or imaginative paintings were still few, but the portrait and the miniature became very fashionable. Rich Elizabethans liked to see records of their features, which also displayed the splendour of their clothes and their status in society. In the miniatures of Nicholas Hilliard, the use of decoration (such as the roses and thorns in that reproduced opposite right) is meant to reveal the feelings and temperament of the subject. Paintings of the Queen, although carefully realistic in some details, portrayed her almost as a religious cult-figure.

The best-remembered Elizabethan achievement was in the field of drama. There was already a popular theatrical tradition, as seen in the mystery and miracle plays, but now noblemen such as the Earl of Leicester

"She [*Elizabeth*] took me to her bed-chamber, and opened a little cabinet, wherein were divers little pictures wrapt within paper, and their names written with her own hand upon the papers. Upon the first that she took up was written, 'My Lord's picture.' I held the candle and pressed to see that picture so named. She appeared loath to let me see it; yet my importunity prevailed for a sight thereof, and found it to be the Earl of Leicester's picture." *Sir James Melville (1535–1617), Memoirs.*

Nicholas Hilliard (1547–1619) was the most
fashionable artist of Elizabeth's reign. Most
of his work consists of miniature portraits,
often sent by lovers to their mistresses. The
symbolic backgrounds of flames (*above left*)
and roses and thorns (*above*) represent the
feelings of the subject. *Left* is a self-portrait in
similar style. See also pages 30 *top left*, 31 *top
left* and 62.

began to assemble companies of actors. Elizabeth herself was a keen patron, and some of William Shakespeare's early plays were performed before her at court as well as in the popular playhouses. Shakespeare's history plays aimed to glorify Elizabeth by showing how her ancestors had achieved their power and prestige, but he went on to produce great tragedies which were enjoyed by the cultured few and by the sensation-hungry populace. Christopher Marlowe, later killed in a public-house brawl, wrote thrilling and spectacular melodramas such as *Doctor Faustus*, while Ben Jonson delicately poked fun at the everyday life of ordinary London people. Perhaps for the last time, the educated nobleman and the poor artisan shared the same tastes in entertainment.

Music flourished, too. Elizabeth kept a court orchestra of eighteen trumpeters, seven violinists, six flautists, six bagpipers and four drummers. Part-songs and madrigals were very popular, and were printed with the music set out on four sides of a square so they could be sung round the table at home. Perhaps the greatest artistic success of Elizabeth's time was the lute song, which brought together the talents of poets such as Sir Philip Sidney, and composers such as John Dowland. Religious music, on the other hand, suffered through the attempts of the Puritans to strip church services bare of all their inessential adornments. Thomas Tallis and William Byrd, however, wrote beautiful settings for the Latin Mass. It shows how highly the composer's art was regarded, that Elizabeth granted these two a monopoly on the sale of printed music for twenty-one years. Music was a social necessity, and learning to read it, as well as to sing and play an instrument, was an essential part of a good education.

The celebrations on Elizabeth's Accession Day took the form of a medieval tournament, but the military skills displayed no longer had any function in real warfare. The court masque emerged as an entertainment uniting the talents of playwrights, musicians and painters. Later it came to be dominated by the spec-

Above Most well-to-do families played music together, and in particular it was an important part of a girl's education.

"**Supper being ended, and the Musicke bookes, according to the custome being brought to the table: the mistresse of the house presented mee with a part, earnestly requesting mee to sing. But when, after many excuses, I protested unfeinedly that I could not: everie one began to wonder. Yea, some whispered to others, demanding how I was brought up.**" *Thomas Morley, Plaine and Easy Introduction to Practicall Musicke, 1597.*

Opposite A striking portrait of Elizabeth at the age of fifty-nine, showing her standing on a globe on Sir Henry Lee's house in Oxfordshire. There she acted in a masque, rather like Sleeping Beauty, playing the heroine who released Sir Henry from his enchanted slumber.

> "Her Majesty mounted the stairs, amid such sounding of trumpets that methought I was on the field of war. As soon as Her Majesty was set at her place, many knights and ladies began a grand ball. When this came to an end, there was a mingled comedy [*Twelfth Night by Shakespeare*], with pieces of music and dances."
>
> *Don Virginio Orsino, Duke of Bracciano, 6th January, 1600.*

tacular scenery designed by architects such as Inigo Jones, but in *Twelfth Night*, written to be performed by the Queen's choristers, Shakespeare overcame the unrealistic setting with some of his most evocative poetry.

Elizabeth, with her usual financial prudence, did not commission any new palaces or other monuments to her architectural taste. The passing out of fashion of the Gothic style brought to an end a great English tradition of religious architecture. But in the large country houses, which for the first time did not need to be equipped for defence, England did evolve a distinc-

tively "Elizabethan" style of building. In this, classical decoration was applied to a basically "perpendicular" structure. This style is seen at its most impressive in Burghley House, near Peterborough, built by Elizabeth's Secretary of State with the wealth he had amassed in office.

Elizabeth's reign was an age of tremendous vitality, when men took a great pride in displaying their achievements in a wide variety of fields. Civilized, educated gentlemen sought to express themselves in thought and in action, in art and in politics, and it was

Above Burghley House. Notice the medieval-style window on the right, the typically Tudor rectangular windows on the main front, and the classical decoration along the roof-line and on the turrets.
Left The Royal Exchange in London, built by Sir Thomas Gresham, a wealthy financier and diplomat. The style is basically Tudor, but there is an Italian classical influence on the central arches and the dormer windows.

The funeral of Sir Philip Sidney. His tenant farmers carry the coffin, his relatives carry the banners, and his friends (including the poet Fulke Greville) hold the corners of the pall.

not thought unusual for a soldier (Sir Philip Sidney) to be a poet, or a sailor (Sir Walter Raleigh) to be a historian. Elizabeth's father, Henry VIII, had himself been a talented composer and musician. Nor was culture confined to the upper classes. At least in the towns, the grammar schools provided a fine education for the sons of craftsmen, and in London the theatre was popular with all except the Puritans. For women, it was not so easy to express themselves other than as wives and mothers: they took almost no part in life outside the home, though many aristocratic ladies had an excellent education. At the summit of Tudor society was Elizabeth herself, a great credit to the standard of education and a discriminating patron of the lively artistic scene.

Sir Walter Raleigh, explorer, historian and poet, later executed for treason under James I, painted with his son in 1602.

14 Society: Problems of Progress

THE DAILY LIFE OF THE QUEEN and her courtiers was obviously vastly different from that of the people. The tastes and manners of the rich had changed a great deal during the previous century under the influence of the Italian Renaissance, and the civilized Elizabethan nobleman, living off his rents and his monopolies, would have had very little in common with his great-grandfather who fought in the Wars of the Roses. For the poor, except in the towns, life had changed much less: indeed there was probably more real hardship, as Henry VIII's dissolution of the monasteries had taken away the protection of the monks' charity. Even so, there were aspects which were common to all Elizabethans.

The concept of personal hygiene was still in its infancy. Medicine was making enormous progress – Shakespeare's son-in-law was an eminent doctor – but at times it bordered on witchcraft. The mortality rate was high, and bubonic plague was a constant worry. Many houses still had open cesspits, and drinking water was drawn from the polluted rivers. Remarkably few people seem to have connected the plague with the insanitary state of the towns and cities, though they did notice they were safer in the country. In this respect men such as Dr. Caius, the second founder of Gonville and Caius College in the University of Cambridge, were rare. His plans for spacious open courts surrounded by low buildings were, for their day, remarkably advanced.

"Next came the Queen, in the sixty-fifth year of her age, as we were told, very majestic; her face oblong, fair, but wrinkled; her eyes small, yet black and pleasant; her nose a little hooked; her lips narrow; and her teeth black (a defect the English seem subject to, from their too great use of sugar); she had in her ears two pearls, with very rich drops; she wore false hair, and that red." *Paul Hentzner, A Journey into England in the Year 1598.*

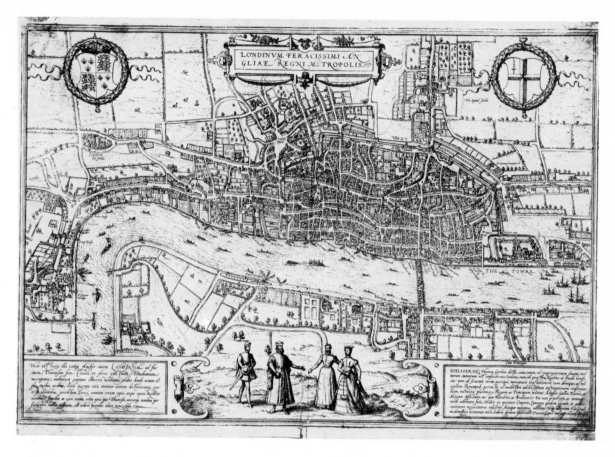

Food was eaten in what seems today vast quantities, though again, the diet of the rich was very different from that of the poor. The peasants ate what they could grow locally, and there was still very little meat or fish in their diets. The well-to-do Elizabethans certainly liked variety in their menus, and were eager to seek out new spices from abroad. Often these were necessary to disguise the taste of decaying foods. They were also fond of sweetmeats, and Elizabeth's teeth were ravaged by her over-indulgence.

Both men and women dressed extravagantly, and children too wore adult clothing in miniature. In fact children were generally treated as miniature adults, and in their childhood, both Elizabeth and her brother

London during Elizabeth's reign. The city was already beginning to grow outside its walls around Smithfield and along the Strand, but Holborn and Bishopsgate were still country lanes lined with orchards and market-gardens. Notice the two theatres on the south bank west of London Bridge.

The Cobhams, a typical wealthy Elizabethan family, painted in 1567. The six children were aged from one to six, and more would probably follow. The dog, the goldfinch, the parrot and the monkey were not an unusually large number of pets, though the last two were rare and expensive imports.

seem to have behaved in a remarkably grown-up fashion by our standards. Although many Puritans thought that all personal adornment was sinful, rich Elizabethans spent a great deal of time and money trying to look their best. The Queen had her wardrobe crammed with elaborate and expensive dresses, many of which she had only worn once. Cosmetics were used liberally, especially by Elizabeth herself as she grew older.

Relations between the sexes were relaxed, and among the aristocracy men and women treated each other as equals. But in principle women were still regarded as inferior, a view which the Bible encouraged. Public life was still wholly dominated by men: but the existence of a female sovereign, and one who so successfully imposed her will on the men around her, helped to create a greater respect for women's abilities.

The pursuit of knowledge was favoured by the settled state of the country, and by increasing prosperity. Although the Renaissance came late to England, it flourished quickly. The old religious centres of education continued to prosper in such places as York and Canterbury, whilst the new grammar schools sprang up through the second half of the sixteenth century. Several, such as those at Blackburn and Halifax, were founded by the Queen herself, while others, among them Merchant Taylor's and Harrow, were endowed by wealthy merchants. People began to take an interest in the past: Shakespeare's plays, for example, show a fascination both with the Greek and Roman origins of European civilization, and with England's medieval past, in particular her monarchs and the growth in their power. The Catholic Church had been a great patron of learning, but it had confined men's thoughts to strictly regulated channels; now, in an age of great self-confidence, when the voyages of discovery were revising the old ideas about the physical world, men such as Francis Bacon, in his *Novum Organum*, were applying the new scientific method to philosophical thought, while in France, Jean Bodin was explaining human society in terms of the law of supply and demand.

It is perhaps surprising that in this ferment of intellectual activity there was not more social unrest and religious strife. Elizabeth had wisely taken much of the heat out of the second issue early in her reign (though controversy raged throughout it), and England was mercifully spared the tragedies of civil war that ravaged other European countries. There was indeed some discontent among the people, but it was produced by par-

Social conflict increased as times became harder in the 1590s, and monopolist courtiers were blamed for adding to the suffering of the poor.

A
QVIP FOR AN VP-
ftart Courtier:
Or,
A quaint difpute betvveen Veluet breeches
and Cloth-breeches.

*Wherein is plainely fet downe the diforders
in all Eftates and Trades.*

LONDON
Imprinted by Iohn Wolfe, and are to bee fold at his
fhop at Poules chayne. 1592.

ticular economic grievances, such as monopolies, rather than any desire to overthrow the government. Although national success in war and naval exploits no doubt made people more contented and less likely to rebel, the fear of a mob uprising was never completely allayed. Elizabeth's laws against vagabondage, for example, which were an attempt to cope with its effects, rather than its causes, seem particularly cruel to us. By placing the responsibility at parish level, the Poor Law of 1601 determined the way the nation treated the very poor, even as late as World War II, and produced the notorious Dickensian workhouses and parish beadles. And yet the Elizabethans, including the Queen herself, could be intensely sentimental and soft-hearted people.

There was little danger of rebellion amongst the common people of the countryside, the peasants and farm workers – they were too ill-organized, and more concerned with local than national events. The London mob was always a threat, as it showed during the Civil War, but Elizabeth took particular care to keep on good terms with the people of her capital. The real danger came from the middle classes, the merchants and country gentlemen, who were important men in their own neighbourhoods but who had little political power. Most of the Members of Parliament came from this class, and Elizabeth, knowing they might turn hostile, treated the House of Commons with great delicacy. She might take no notice of what they had to say, but she usually listened politely to their addresses. James I and Charles I, her successors, were less skilful and more tactless. Less than forty years after her death, a movement which had begun with mild protests against particular grievances had become an attack on the whole system of government.

15 The New Century

THE LAST FEW YEARS OF THE CENTURY – and her reign – saw the death of many of Elizabeth's devoted servants. Drake died in January, 1596, and Lord Keeper Puckering shortly after. Hunsdon, the Lord Chamberlain, died the same year, as well as Sir Francis Knollys, Treasurer of the Household, and Blanche Parry, who had been a companion of Elizabeth since childhood. In 1598 it was the turn of Lord Burghley. As he lay dying he offered to resign his offices, but with the deep sympathy of which she was often capable, Elizabeth realized that he wished to die her Treasurer. She even visited his bedside and fed him herself. It was not his fault that he had no time left to carry out the reforms that he could see were urgently needed. He had fashioned the office of Secretary of State almost on his own, and would doubtless have brought the same qualities to that of Treasurer, had he been appointed sooner.

Even without the loss of such men, there were many other factors to darken the closing years of her reign – factors over which Elizabeth had little or no direct control. The economic consequences of the war with Spain were making themselves keenly felt: taxes were high, overseas trade was disrupted, and the value of money was dropping – the process which we know today as inflation, but which was then imperfectly understood. There were outbreaks of plague; men were pressed into military service, and there was a run of bad harvests. The popularity of Elizabeth herself, which had been at its zenith in the years immediately after the Armada, now began to wane.

This loss of popularity was vividly demonstrated

"Incredible was the kindness which Queen Elizabeth had for him [*Burghley*], or rather for herself in him, being sensible that he was so able a minister of state. Coming once to visit him, being sick of the gout ... and being much heightened with her head attire (then in fashion) the lord's servant who conducted her through the door, 'May your highness,' said he, 'be pleased to stoop.'
The queen returned, 'For your master's sake I will stoop, but not for the King of Spain's.'"
Thomas Fuller, The English Worthies, 1662.

"Her wisest men and best councillors were oft sore troubled to know her will in matters of state, so covertly [*secretly*] did she pass her judgement." *Sir John Harington (1561–1612), Nugae Antiquae.*

Right Epidemics of plague were a constant threat, especially in the overcrowded and unhealthy City of London. This picture was drawn in the early seventeenth century.

Below There was a revival of interest in alchemy during Elizabeth's reign, especially in trying to turn base metals such as lead into gold.

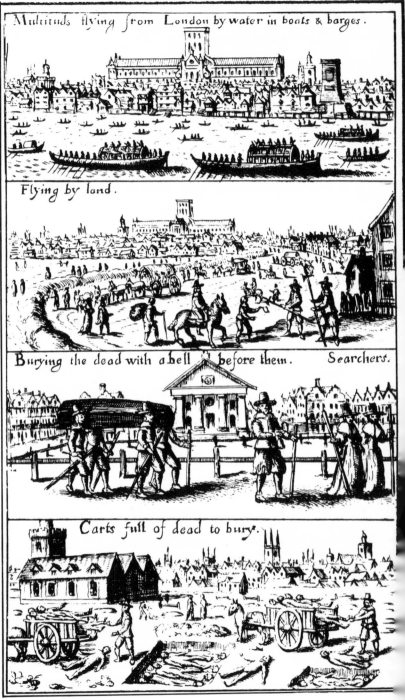

Multituds flying from London by water in boats & barges.

Flying by land.

Burying the dead with a bell before them.   Searchers.

Carts full of dead to bury.

when Elizabeth came to open Parliament at the end of
October, 1602. Very few members were heard to say
"God save your Majesty"; few even made room for her,
when the ushers called out for them to do so. She needed
Parliament to grant more taxes to meet the costs of the
war with Spain and the fighting in Ireland, but before
voting her any money the Commons wanted to discuss
the burning issue of monopolies. In the previous session
Elizabeth had promised to do something about this
crying scandal, but had failed to do so. The granting of
a monopoly in the sale of, for instance, raisins or spices,
was a useful way of handing out rewards for services
rendered, and was the Queen's prerogative – Parliament had no right to any say in the matter. In such
difficult times it had therefore become all the more
useful, since it cost nothing. It was not at all popular,
since the monopolist, often a nobleman trying to maintain a lavish style of life at a time when his income from
rents was falling, could charge what he liked for his
goods. Elizabeth was not anxious for the matter to be
aired, therefore, and since it touched her prerogative,
she guarded it all the more jealously.

Elizabeth might have been losing her popularity in
some quarters, but she had not lost her political skill.
She sent for the Speaker, for him to convey a message
to the House. In it she thanked them for making "so
hasty and free a subsidy" – which they had not in fact
done – and promised a proclamation about monopolies,
which was actually published within a matter of days.
Far from being an ogre, Elizabeth now emerged as a
fairy godmother. The Commons wanted to thank her,
and by way of reply she delivered what has become
known as her Golden Speech. The Commons responded
by granting her the subsidies she needed for the next
four years, so she was unlikely to summon another
Parliament during her lifetime. At sixty-eight she
certainly had not lost her touch.

Elizabeth went to the Lords in person for the dissolution of Parliament before the Christmas recess, and the
speech she made on that occasion was virtually a sum-

"Though God hath raised me
high, yet this I account the glory
of my crown, that I have reigned
with your loves. . . . It is not my
desire to live or reign longer
than my life and reign shall be
for your good. And though you
have had, and may have, many
mightier and wiser princes
sitting in this seat, yet you never
had, nor shall have, any that will
love you better." *Queen Elizabeth's
Golden Speech to Parliament, 30th
November, 1601.*

ming up of her policies during the forty-four years of her reign. Much of it was concerned with her foreign policy, and the fact that she had never sought glory for herself when she involved the country in war abroad: "I have diminished my own revenue that I might add to your security and been content to be a taper of virgin wax to waste myself and spend my life that I might give light and comfort to those that live under me."

Perhaps most notable in the speech was its omission of any reference to the succession. Many people were worried that James VI of Scotland might face a rebellion, or an attack from Spain, on his accession, but Elizabeth continued to appear confident. It was yet another topic that she refused to consider as the concern of Parliament, or of anyone else unless she chose to raise the question. She knew that her death might not be far off, and that some people in her employment were already in contact with her successor across the Border. Was it simply that she felt sure that nothing would upset the order of things, or was it that she scarcely cared any more, and so decided to let events take their course, for better or for worse? If trouble lay ahead, then it would be for another to deal with. She was too old, tired and lonely.

Opposite James VI of Scotland and I of England, who was in correspondence with English nobles and statesmen for many years before Elizabeth's death.

"As for me, I see no such great cause why I should either be fond to live or fear to die. I have had good experience of this world, and I know what it is to be a subject and what to be a sovereign. Good neighbours I have had, and I have met with bad: and in trust I have found treason." *Queen Elizabeth to Parliament, 1586.*

16 Time for a change

ELIZABETH DIED AT RICHMOND at about three o'clock in the morning of 24th March, 1603, from the complications that followed a bad cold. Her godson, Sir John Harington, who had seen her the previous Christmas at Whitehall, said then that she "doth now bear show of human infirmity too fast for that evil which we shall get by her death, and too slow for that good which we shall get by her releasement from her pains and misery." Harington found her "in a most pitiable state." though when she asked him about his writing and he read some of his poetry to her, she remarked rather tartly, "When thou dost feel creeping Time at thy gate, these fooleries will please thee less. I am past relish for such matters." Astonishingly, she appeared to the Venetian ambassador at the beginning of February in silver and white taffeta trimmed with gold, and with jewels everywhere. She then upbraided him, in Italian, because Venice had never sent a diplomatic representative to her court until this, the forty-fifth – and last – year of her reign.

No other monarch since Edward III had reigned for so long. As the playwright Thomas Dekker said in his lament for her, she "brought up (even under her wing) a nation that was almost begotten and born under her." Whatever the faults of Elizabeth as a person, or of her government of the country, particularly since her triumph over the Armada, she gave the English people a feeling of nationhood, and saved them from the agony of civil and religious war, thus giving her country time to grow and put down roots. When greeted by a pageant with the figure of Time in her coronation procession,

"Must! Is *must* a word to be addressed to princes? Little man, little man! thy father, if he had been alive, durst not have used that word. Ye know that I must die, and that makes ye so presumptuous." *Queen Elizabeth, on her death-bed, to Burghley's son Robert Cecil.*

"She was strangely attired in a dress of silver cloth, white and crimson, or silver 'gauze,' as they call it. This dress had slashed sleeves lined with red taffeta, and was girt about with other little sleeves, that hung down to the ground, which she was for ever twisting and untwisting. She kept the front of her dress open, and one could see the whole of her bosom, and passing low, and often she would open the front of this robe with her hands as if she was too hot." *De Maisse, Ambassador from Henri IV of France, 1597.*

Opposite In this painting, made in about 1600, Elizabeth is at last shown as an old woman, but she still wears her traditional finery, and faces the threat of death calmly.

Above and right Queen Elizabeth's funeral. A carved effigy of the Queen was placed on top of the coffin. Behind is the horse that she had ridden on state occasions.

she remarked: "And Time hath brought me hither." When she came to the throne, England needed time above all else. It was sadly ironical that she eventually became, in Sir Walter Raleigh's words, "a lady whom time hath surprised."

The word Tudor is generally used to describe the England of the sixteenth century, but of the five Tudor sovereigns, only Elizabeth has given her name to an era. The word Elizabethan at once conjures up an age when spring became early summer and seemed to stay that way for at least half a century. There were brave soldiers and sailors, wise statesmen, gifted musicians, artists and writers and, for the most part, a zest for living that was scarcely to be equalled in succeeding ages.

Of course, not all the credit can be given to Elizabeth. The liberating effect on men's minds of the Renaissance and the Reformation, the excitement of new discoveries in geography and science, and the prosperity which brought leisure and education within reach of a larger class, were factors over which she had no control. Unquestionably there was something latent in the spirit of the times, and she was able to set the flame alight. She had a striking personality that demanded admiration even when it provoked criticism. As a

The Earle of Worcester Master of the Horse leading the Palfrey of Estate, two Esquires &c are attending to lead him away.

A Gentleman Usher of the privy chamber

William Dethick Garter Principall King of Armes.

The Lady Marchionesse of Northampton Principall Mourner assisted by the lord Buckhurst Lord Treasurer and the Earle of Nottingham Lord Admirall.

Her trayne assisted by two Countesses and Sr John Stanhop Vice-chamblaine.

superior she must have been frequently infuriating, and it was inevitable that as her old and trusted friends and counsellors disappeared, she should seem less sympathetic, perhaps, and less worthy of respect in the eyes of the rising generation. For them she was the only monarch they had ever known, and such prolonged petticoat rule must have been hard to bear. Yet later generations would have good cause to observe the anniversary of her accession as a day of national celebration, and talk with pride and affection of Good Queen Bess.

Principal Characters

ALENÇON, HERCULE-FRANÇOIS, DUKE OF (1554–84). Sixth and youngest son of Henri II of France and Catherine de' Medici. One of the most likely and persistent suitors for the hand of Elizabeth. Became Duke of Anjou in 1574 when his brother Henri III became king.

ANNE BOLEYN (1507–36). Second wife of Henry VIII and mother of Elizabeth. She married the king secretly before his first marriage was declared null. When she failed to produce a son, she was accused of adultery and incest, and executed on Tower Green.

BURGHLEY, LORD (1520–98). William Cecil was knighted in 1551, conformed to Catholicism in Mary's reign, but stayed in contact with Elizabeth. On her accession he became Secretary of State (responsible for foreign policy), and in 1572 Lord High Treasurer. His son Robert Cecil held high offices under Elizabeth and James I.

DRAKE, SIR FRANCIS (1540?–96). The second man to sail round the world (1577–80), he was knighted by Elizabeth on board the *Golden Hind* on his return. Though not in overall command, he led the destruction of the Spanish Armada. He died at Porto Bello on a treasure-seeking mission to the West Indies.

ESSEX, ROBERT DEVEREUX, EARL OF (1566–1601). He distinguished himself at Zutphen in 1586 and Cadiz in 1596, became a protégé of Elizabeth, and was made Earl Marshal and Chancellor of Cambridge University. He failed to subdue the Irish rebels, tried to stage a coup d'état, and was tried and executed.

JAMES VI OF SCOTLAND AND I OF ENGLAND (1566–1625). Son of Mary Queen of Scots and Lord Darnley, he became King when his mother was deposed by the nobles in 1567, and began his personal rule in 1583. Elizabeth never recognized him as her successor, but she schooled him by letter.

LEICESTER, ROBERT DUDLEY, EARL OF (1532?–88). Elizabeth's chief favourite, perhaps the only man she ever loved, despite his three marriages, one of them bigamous. He fell from favour for accepting the governorship of the Netherlands, but returned to lead the land forces against the Armada.

MARY STUART, QUEEN OF SCOTS (1542–87). Brought up in France and wife of François II, after his death she returned to Scotland. She was hated by the nobles and the Puritans, and twice married foolishly, first Henry, Lord Darnley, and then his murderer James Bothwell. In 1568 she fled to England and spent eighteen years in various prisons before Elizabeth consented to her execution.

PHILIP II, KING OF SPAIN (1527–98). He married Mary Tudor in 1554 and succeeded his father, Charles V, in 1556. He was a hard-working recluse and a fanatical Catholic, who overstrained Spain's resources by fighting the Protestants in England, France and the Netherlands, as well as the Turks. After the defeat of the Armada Spain declined as a great power.

RALEIGH, SIR WALTER (1552–1618). He sailed to America with Sir Humphrey Gilbert in 1578, and repeatedly tried to set up colonies there. He introduced potatoes and tobacco to England, and became a patron of the arts and a leading figure at court. In the 1590s he took part in the Plantation of Ulster with Protestant settlers. Under James I he was arrested for treason, wrote a *History of the World* in prison, and was eventually beheaded.

WALSINGHAM, SIR FRANCIS (1536–89). He helped Burghley to expose the Ridolfi plot, and in 1573 succeeded him as Secretary of State. He acted as an ambassador to Scotland, France and the Netherlands. He was one of the few Elizabethan ministers who did not take bribes, but he has been accused of manufacturing evidence to trap the Babington Conspirators.

Table of Dates

1517   Martin Luther's ninety-five theses – start of the Reformation.

1529   Henry VIII sues for divorce.

1533   Birth of Elizabeth.
       Act of Supremacy.

1536   Execution of Anne Boleyn.

1539   Dissolution of the monasteries.

1545   Council of Trent – start of the Counter-Reformation.

1547   Henry VIII dies. Edward VI becomes King.

1553   Edward VI dies. Northumberland proclaims Lady Jane Grey as Queen. Mary in fact succeeds.

1554   Mary marries Philip of Spain.
       Elizabeth arrested after Wyatt's rebellion.

1555   Peace of Augsburg – end of religious wars in Germany.
       Charles V abdicates. Philip II becomes King of Spain.

1558   Mary dies. Elizabeth becomes Queen.

1559   Treaty of Cateau-Cambrésis – peace between France and Spain.
       Acts of Uniformity and Supremacy.

1566   Revolt of the Netherlands begins.
       Murder of Riccio. James VI and I born.

1568   Mary Stuart escapes to England.

1570   Pope Pius V excommunicates Elizabeth. Ridolfi Plot.

1572   Massacre of St. Bartholomew's Day.
       Elizabeth expels the Sea Beggars.
       Treaty of Blois between England and France.

Opposite A broadsheet published shortly after Elizabeth's death, showing in the centre scenes from conspiracies and risings against the Queen, and around the outside the fates of the traitors and rebels. The Gunpowder Plot against James I is also illustrated (no. 16).

POPISH PLOTS
AND
TREASONS

First are describ'd the Cursed plots the
laid.
And on the side their wretched ends dis
play'd.

from the beginning of the Reign of Queen Elizabeth-
Illustrated with Emblems and explain'd in Verse.

Figure 1.

The Pope aloft on Armed Shoulders Rides,
And in a ring Hopes the English spoils divides;
Rebellion bald spirit good Bulls roares,
Scatters dire Rebellion round our shoars,
Which blesses the Villains, Cheats them on,
promise Heav'n Crown, when her Crowns won,
God doth blast their Troops, their Counsels mock,
And brings bald Traitors to th' deserved Block,

Figure 3.

A King, and Romes Triple-Crown'd Pelate Joyn,
with them both bold Stukely does Combine
to conquer, And the Pope his tool,
at Bleisworck, as Holy Regiment;
their way at Barbery they call,
at one Blow the Moore destroy them All.
here, what Ambition Traitors Gain,
shame of Christian is by Pagans Slain.

Figure 5.

truly Janizaries are Monks to Rome,
their dark Cells the blackest Treasons come.
Popes Licence horrid Crimes they Act,
build with piety each Treacherous Fact.
every Priest, like Comets Blaze,
always Blood shed and Rebellion Raise;
till the fatal Gibbet's ready feet
such, where Treason's with Religion mixt.

Figure 7.

Spanish Embassador here Leiger lies,
are laid the English to surprize;
theologies is Secretary had Got
power to effect the Hellish Plot.
our Havens Names, where Foes might Land,
what Papists were to lend an hand,
a base Trick he's forc'd to pack to Spain
Tyburn greets confederates that remain.

Figure 9.

vile Doctrines do Convince
Merit for to kill his Prince,
Dagger he prepares with Art,
to sheath it in her Royal Heart,
temps, and is as oft put by,
jestick Terrors of her Eye;
Cursed Intentions he Confest
his welcom'd a fit Tyburn Guest;

Figure 11.

with Spain alone, Great Betty's Strife,
attempts upon her pretious Life;
cause th' Ambassador to Bribe
others, of the Roman Tribe;
off. To which they soon Consent,
Heav'n does that Guilt prevent.
doth to the Councel All Disclose,
with shame perfidious Mounsieur goes.

Figure 13.

private horrid Treason view
the Pope, the Devil, and a Jew;
tor must by Poison do
Plots have laid in hitherto:
begins method, the Judas Cries;
and Crowns, t' other replies,
but hold, the wretch shall miss his hope,
known, and his Reward's the Rope.

Figure 15.

James had blest the English Throne,
Priests Conspire to pull him down.
sonous Maximes does Instill,
some Nobles to Join in the Ill;
when appear the most divine,
with unexpected Mercy Shine.
fatal Ax attempts the Stroke,
ins in and does the Blow Revoke,

us, with cheerful Hymns of praise,
land'd with love an Altar raise
to God, who doth advance
Arm to our Deliverance,
that doth protect his Sheep,
this poor Island keep
Wolves, which would as soon devour,
by his mighty power,
with our Church, with freedome Crown,
Popish Superstitions down,
and may they never rise,
Remember our Eyes;
whose mercies ever are most tender
our Faith, and Faiths Defender.

IN NOMINE
DOMINI
incipit Omne Malum

A THANKFVLL
REMEMBRANCE
OF GODS MERCIE
by

Deo Liberatori   Deo Reduci

Sold by John Garret at his Shop, at the Exchange
Staires in Cornhill, where you may have choice
of all Sorts of Large and Small Maps: Draw-
ing Books Coppy books, and Pictures for Gen-
tlewomens works: and also very good origi-
nals of French and Dutch Prints.

Figure 2.

Don John, who under Spain did with proud Hand
The then unsever'd Netherlands Command,
Conceives for Englands Conquest, and does Hope
To Gain is by Donation from the Pope,
Yet to Amuse our Queen does still pretend
perpetual peace, and needs will seem a friend;
But Heav'n looks through those Juggles and in's prime
Grief Cuts off Him and's Hopes All at a time.

Figure 4.

The Priests, with Crosses Ensigne-like display'd,
Prompt bloody Desmond to those spoiles he made
On Irish Protestants, and from afar
Blow Triumphs to Rebellions Holy War;
But against Providence all Arts are vain,
The Crafty, in their Craft are over-tane;
Behold where kill'd the Stubborn Traitor lies,
Whilst to the Woods his Ghostly Father flies;

Figure 6.

Mad Sommervil, by Cruel Priests inspir'd
To do whatever mischiefe they requir'd,
Swears that he instantly will be the death
Of good and Gracious Queen Elizabeth.
Assaults her Guards, but Heav'n protecting pow'r
Defeats his rage makes him a Prisoner:
Where to avoid a just, though shameful Death,
Self-strangling hands do Stop his loathsome breath.

Figure 8.

View here a Miracle —— A Priest Conveys,
In Spanish Bottom o're the path-less Seas,
Close treacherous Notes, whilst a Dutch Ship comes
And freight Engag'd her well-known Enemy:
The Conscious Priest his Guilty Papers tears,
And over board the scatter'd fragments bears;
But the just winds do force them back o'th' Decks,
And peice-meal all the lurking plot detects.

Figure 10.

Here Babington and all his desperate Band,
Ready prepar'd for Royal Murder stand,
His Motto seems to glory in the Deed,
These my Companions are whom dangers lead,
Cowardly Traitors, to many Combine
To Cut off one poor Ladies vital Twine;
In vain,—— Heav'n's her Guard, and as for you;
Behold, the Hangman gives you all your due.

Figure 12.

Spain's proud Armada, whom the Pope did bless,
Attacques our Isle, Confident of success,
But Heav'ns just Blast doth Scatter all their force,
They fly and quite round Scotland take their Course;
So many taken, burnt, and Sunk i'th' Main,
Scarce one Tenth liv'd to get home Again;
Thus England like Noahs Ark, amidst the Waves
Indulgent providence from Danger saves.

Figure 14.

The Great Tyrone that did so oft embrew
Ireland with Blood, and Popish Plots Renew;
Here vanquisht Swears, upon his bended knee,
To the Queens Deputy fidelity.
Yet breaks that vow, and loaded with the Guilt
Of perjuries and Blood which he had spilt.
Being forc'd at last to fly his Native Land,
Carries in's Breast a sting, a Scourge in's hand

Figure 16.

In this Curs'd Powder-plot we plainly see
The Quintessence of Romish Cruelty.
King Lords and Commons at one Hellish Blast
Had been destroy'd, and half our Land laid wast,
See Faux, with his dark Lanthorn, ready stands
To Light the fatal Train with desperate hands,
But Heavens All-seeing eye defeats their desire,
And saves us as a Brand snatcht from the fire;

Let us to both a strict Adherence pay,
And for their preservation ever pray,
Since this Truths happy Bark hath reach'd our sho
O may it never, never Leave us more.

1577	Drake sails round the world.
	Suppression of Puritan "prophesyings".
1585	Elizabeth sends troops to the Netherlands.
	Founding of Virginia in America.
1586	Babington Plot uncovered.
1587	Mary Queen of Scots executed.
	Drake's raid on Cadiz.
1588	Defeat of the Spanish Armada.
	Death of the Earl of Leicester.
1589	Henri of Navarre becomes King of France.
1591	Elizabeth sends troops to help Henri IV of France.
1596	Rebellion in Ireland.
1598	Philip II of Spain dies.
	Treaty of Vervins ends French and Dutch wars.
	Edict of Nantes gives toleration to French Protestants.
	Death of Lord Burghley.
1599	Essex's expedition to Ireland.
1601	Essex's rebellion and execution.
	Foundation of East India Company.
	New Poor Law passed.
1603	Death of Queen Elizabeth.
	James VI of Scotland becomes James I of England.

Picture Credits

The author and publishers wish to thank the following for permission to reproduce copyright illustrations appearing on the pages mentioned: the Marquess of Salisbury, *Frontispiece*, 30 *top right*; Radio Times Hulton Picture Library, 8 *top*, 27, 34, 39, 45, 46–7, 50, 53, 56, 84; National Portrait Gallery, 8 *bottom*, 18, 24, 30 left and bottom right, 31, 70, 75; Mary Evans Picture Library, 10, 12, 14, 36, 59; Mrs. Dent-Brocklehurst, 17; John Freeman & Co., 23, 44, 48, 52, 64, 74, 79, 93; British Museum, 26, 40, 41, 63, 88, 89; Mansell Collection, 28; Courtauld Institute, 55, 67; Lord Cowdray, 61; Victoria and Albert Museum, 69; the Marquess of Exeter, 73; London Museum, 77; the Marquess of Bath, 78; Lord Methuen and A. C. Cooper Ltd., 86. Other pictures are from the Wayland Picture Library.

Further Reading

The most informative and reliable biography of Elizabeth is *Elizabeth I*, by Sir John Neale (Jonathan Cape 1934). A more up-to-date book, in a more popular style, is *Elizabeth, Queen of England* by Neville Williams (Weidenfeld and Nicolson 1967). Two fascinating works dealing with the Queen's relations with her most effective minister and her temperamental young favourite are *Lord Burghley and Queen Elizabeth*, by Conyers Read (Jonathan Cape 1960), and *Elizabeth and Essex*, by Lytton Strachey (Chatto and Windus 1928). The Queen's own writing, of which not very much survives, is collected in *The Letters of Queen Elizabeth*, edited by G. B. Harrison (Cassell 1935; out of print).

A simple introduction to the political history of the period is *Elizabeth I and the Unity of England*, by Joel Hurstfield (E.U.P. 1960). A more detailed look at one aspect of the reign which affected every problem of government is provided in *Elizabeth and her Parliaments*, by Sir John Neale (Jonathan Cape 1953).

A great many books have been written about Elizabethan culture and society. Among those suitable for children are *Shakespeare's England*, by Levi Fox (Wayland 1972), and *English Life in Tudor Times*, by Roger Hart (Wayland 1972). Finally, A. L. Rowse has written a number of stimulating books about the period, though some historians disagree strongly with many of his ideas; the two most useful are *The England of Elizabeth: the Structure of Society* (Macmillan 1950), and *The Elizabethan Renaissance* (2 vols., Macmillan 1971–72).

Available in paperback.

Index

Alva, Duke of 35–6
Anabaptists 19
Architecture 72–3
Armada, Spanish 42–8
Ashley, Kate 11

Babington, Anthony 38
Bacon, Francis 79
Blois, Treaty of 66
Boleyn, Anne 8, 9, 90
Burghley House, Peterborough 73
Byrd, William 71

Cadiz, Spain 42–3, 58
Calais, France 15, 20, 45, 58
Calvin, John 16
Campion, Edmund 52
Cateau-Cambrésis, Treaty of 20
Catherine de' Medici, Queen of France 20, 28
Catholicism 7, 8, 13, 14, 16–19, 27, 50, 52, 55
Cecil, William Lord Burghley 18, 36, 40, 67, 73, 81, 90
Charles V, Holy Roman Emperor 8, 13
Charles IX, King of France 20, 28
Clifford, George Earl of Cumberland 62
Cobham family 78
Costume, Elizabethan 9, 30–1, 32, 61, 62, 69, 77–8, 87
Cranmer, Thomas Archbishop of Canterbury 15

Darnley, Henry Lord 25–6
Dekker, Thomas 87
Devereux, Robert Earl of Essex 32, 56, 57–9, 90
Dowland, John 71
Drake, Francis 34, 36, 42–3, 57, 61, 65, 81, 90
Drama 61, 71
Dudley, Guildford 11
Dudley, John Duke of Northumberland 11
Dudley, Robert Earl of Leicester 32, 33, 37, 57, 68, 91

East India Company 65, 66
Education, Elizabethan 9–10, 74, 79
Edward VI, King of England 9, 10, 11, 17
Eric, King of Sweden 28

Farnese, Alexander, Prince of Parma 36, 42
Fotheringhay Castle, Northamptonshire 39, 40–41
France 7, 15, 19, 20, 28, 35, 57, 66–7
François II, King of France 20

Grey, Lady Jane 11, 13
Grindal, Edmund 50, 52–3

Hampton Court, Middlesex 15
Harington, John 87
Hatfield 9, 11, 15
Hawkins, John 36, 42, 61, 65
Henri II, King of France 20
Henri, Duke of Anjou (later Henri III, King of France) 28, 40
Henri IV, King of France 57, 67
Henry VIII, King of England 8, 10, 17, 74
Hepburn, James Earl of Bothwell 26
Hercule-François, Duke of Alençon 28, 37, 90
Hilliard, Nicholas 30, 31, 62, 68, 69
Holinshed, Raphael 7
Hooker, Richard 50
Howard of Effingham, Lord 43, 45, 58, 67
Huguenots 20–1, 51

Ireland 59–60

James V, King of Scotland 25
James VI of Scotland and I of England 22, 25, 32, 40–41, 80, 84, 85, 90
Jones, Inigo 72
Jonson, Ben 61, 71

Katherine of Aragon 8

Latimer, Hugh, Bishop 10
Le Havre, France 20
London 77, 82; Chelsea 10; Essex House 60; Globe Theatre 60; Greenwich Palace (Placentia) 7; Royal Exchange 72; St Margaret's Church, Westminster 61; St Paul's Cathedral 48; Whitehall Palace 12
Luther, Martin 8

Marlowe, Christopher 61, 71
Marprelate Tracts 49
Mary of Guise 25
Mary Stuart, Queen of Scotland 7, 18, 24, 25, 26, 27, 32, 38–41, 91
Mary Tudor, Queen of England 7–9, 11, 12, 13–16, 17, 50, 52
Medina Sidonia, Duke of 44
Monopolies 83
Mountjoy, Lord 60
Music 71

Navy, British 42–3, 45, 58
Netherlands, the 19, 21, 28, 35–7, 66–7
Nonsuch Palace 59

Norfolk, Duke of 27
Norris, John 57

O'Neill, Hugh Earl of Tyrone 59

Painting 30–1, 68–9
Parker, Matthew 49, 50
Parliament 22, 23, 33, 39, 67, 83–5
Parr, Catherine 9, 11, 32
Parry, Blanche 81
Philip II, King of Spain 12, 13–5, 17, 35, 41–2, 58, 91
Poor Law (1601) 65, 80
Popes: Clement VIII 8; Pius V 27
Portraits of Elizabeth 2, 6, 28–9, 30–1, 33, 39, 61, 70, 86
Privy Council 40
Protestantism 7, 8, 16–9, 35
Puritans 18, 49–55

Raleigh, Walter 65, 74, 75, 88, 91
Reformation 8, 14
Renaissance 61–4, 68, 79
Riccio, David 25
Richmond 87
Ridolfi Plot 27
Robsart, Amy 32

St Bartholomew Massacre 21, 28, 51
Scotland 25–6
Sea Beggars 35–6, 66
Seymour: Edward Duke of Somerset 10–11; Henry 43; Jane 9; Thomas, Lord High Admiral 11
Shakespeare, William 61, 71, 79; Richard II 60; Twelfth Night 72
Sidney, Philip 54, 55, 71, 74
Spain 15, 21, 36, 40, 42–8, 58–9, 66
Spenser, Edmund 54
Star Chamber 60
Stubbes, John 54
Supremacy, Act of 16

Tallis, Thomas 71
Tilbury, Essex 48
Tudor, Margaret 25

Uniformity, Act of 16

Walsingham, Francis 27, 38, 39, 91
Whitgift, John 49, 50, 53–4
William, Prince of Orange 35, 37
Windsor Castle, Berkshire 9
Woodstock, Oxfordshire 14
Wyatt, Thomas 14

Figures in *italic* type refer to the illustrations